More in Anger

also by Marya Mannes

MESSAGE FROM A STRANGER

J. B. Lippincott Company : Philadelphia : New York

MORE IN ANGER

MARYA MANNES

Printed in the United States of America
by H. Wolff, New York
Library of Congress Catalog Card Number 58–12279
DESIGN: Marshall Lee
Third Impression

CONTENTS

INTRODUCING MYSELF : *11*

I THE WAY WE ARE: THE RITUALS OF
EQUALITY

1 I'M AS GOOD AS YOU ARE : *21*

2 SMILE, SMILE, SMILE : *25*

3 TWO TYRANNIES : *28*
  "Haven't You Lost Weight, Dear?" : *29*
  Stay Young : *33*

4 THE HALF-PEOPLE : *38*

5 WASTELAND : *40*

6 KEEP OUT THE AIR : *42*

7 THE PATIO AND THE PRIVATE LIFE : *45*
  Gutter Girl or *I Made My Bed* : *46*
  Miltown Place or *Life With Sponsors* : *50*

II POLITICS AND PREJUDICES

1 THE VIEWS OF THE SPEAKER DO NOT
NECESSARILY REPRESENT . . . : 55

2 FANTASY: INAUGURAL SPEECH, 1960 : 66

3 HANDBOOK OF SUBVERSION : 70

4 UNAMERICAN AFFAIRS : 76
Public Servant : 78
The Brotherhood of Hate: Three Portraits : 82
*The Friendliest People in the World,
Fundamentally* : 91

III THE ARTS: SELLING THE PUBLIC

1 THE SMALL SCREEN
The Magic Box : 99
The Child Before the Set : 108
The Victors and the Victims : 113

LADY CHATTERER'S LOVERS : 113
NO KIDDING : 117

2 THE BIG PRETENSIONS : *121*
    Soul for Sale : *125*
    Dissonant Dialogue : *134*
    Dance Lover : *140*

3 ARBITERS OF TASTE : *143*

IV PERSONAL HERESIES

1 SUBJECTIVELY YOURS : *151*

2 LETTER TO A GIRL : *154*

3 IF I WERE A MAN : *160*

4 "OUR AMERICAN WOMEN ARE WONDERFUL,"
    THE AMERICAN SAID SADLY : *164*

5 THE CASE OF THE TWO-HEADED WOMAN : *168*
    Lady Editor : *174*
    The Marriage : *178*

6 MEDITATIONS IN AN EMPTY ROOM : *182*

INTRODUCING MYSELF

When someone comparatively unknown to the public chooses to address it, that public has the right to ask three questions: Who are you? What qualifies you to express your opinions? Why did you write this?

I would like to answer all three, because they bear heavily on what follows in this book and the attitudes taken in it.

I am an American whose grandparents emigrated respectively from Germany and Poland in the nineteenth century. My mother was brought here as an infant, my father was born in New York. Both were musicians, although humanity came before profession: what they gave to their music they gave doubly to my brother and me. I grew up with a profound respect for creative effort and a constant awareness of the disciplines and joys involved in it. My parents gave me, by word and example, inflexible standards of probity, a hatred of cruelty and hypocrisy, a love of Christ, a conviction of the divinity in man, and a conscience which strenuously resists the numerous efforts I have made throughout my life to still it. They presented an ideal from which I have often fallen far short but which I cannot and will not relinquish. It is the basis for the anger which largely impelled this book, for to know the good is to react against the bad. Indifference is the mark of deprivation.

I am certainly not young, neither am I old, although I have lived through the twenties, thirties and forties of this century with the same share of luck and error, of delight and anguish, allotted to most people; and possibly with deeper involvement than many. I consider myself a late developer, having arrived only in mid-life at some sort of plateau of perception from which a coherent pattern at last begins to emerge. I do not think this can be reached without error, without grief, and without failure.

What qualifies me to express my opinions on a variety of subjects on which I cannot call myself an expert? Well, I have been writing for over twenty-five years with one purpose: to communicate clearly and honestly what I see and what I believe about the world I live in. This world is so rich and so varied that out of a blend of curiosity, ebullience and audacity, I have not been able to confine myself, as wise people do, to any single aspect of it. A large element of worldly success is, I believe, just this self-limitation: the channeling of talent and energy in one direction rather than its dispersal in several. If this is true, then success will not be my lot. But I do not want it badly enough to curtail my instincts for exploration, not only of truth but of the different ways in which it can be expressed: oblique and direct, satirical and compassionate, serious and irreverent. You will find, therefore, in this book a considerable change of writing pace, from essay to dialogue, from letter to sketch, from straight criticism to analysis by example. In each case the content has dictated the form.

You will discover too—and perhaps disconcertingly—

that although I make my politics clear I fail to fit neatly into any social or artistic categories. Conservatives will undoubtedly shout "liberal!" but the more militant liberals in both art and politics will in the same breath cry "reactionary!" Professionally I appear to fall uneasily between the writers who succeed because they appeal to the mass audience and those who succeed because they appeal to a superior intellectual elite. The big magazines find me too special and controversial to handle, and the critical literary fraternity find me too explicit to be important.

Although I have read a great deal since the age of five and continue to do so, I cannot, moreover, call myself an intellectual for the simple reason that I have not learned enough. There are gaps in my knowledge of the works of man in every age of which I am acutely aware, the more acutely in the company of the really educated. Yet, though I never went to a university, the ten years I spent in a school run by a Frenchwoman in New York gave me certain disciplines for which I am everlastingly grateful. These included a solid acquaintance with Latin and French, an attitude towards the English language compounded equally of respect and love, and an abiding aversion towards sloppiness and obscurity. My only other education has come from living, working, and learning the lives—through voyages and sojourns abroad since childhood—of other people than my own. Towards this end a familiarity with several languages has stood me in good stead. I comfort myself with the thought that, unimpressive as these qualifications are, many published pages have been written by people with even lesser ones.

Why did I write this book? Because I am angry. Because I have been angry for a long time. With what? With the progressive blurring of American values, the sapping of American strength, the withering of American courage. I think we have been suffering for some time from a sort of spiritual leukemia: an invasion by the white cells of complacency and accommodation; and I cannot mutely observe its dangerous course.

Everything I have seen about me in these last years points to fear, fragmentation, and softness. These were not the qualities that made us great and they are certainly not the qualities that will keep us great.

And if I choose not to celebrate here the virtues which we still possess, it is because they have been accepted too long as fixed attributes of our national character. Friendliness, generosity, ingenuity, diligence, drive, vitality, shrewdness are all admirable traits. But we have congratulated ourselves on them so consistently that they have become a shield, automatically raised, against question. All our mass media are troubadours of these virtues, and the trademark of the nation has come to be a family group gathered around a tray of soft drinks, a smile on each soft face and a barbecue pit in the background to proclaim the soft life. And if you say that these people are merely the projections of the advertising mind, I will answer that nature has copied art and that we are beginning to look like our pictures: dull, amiable, with an appetite for things and none for ideas, a people overnourished physically and undernourished in mind and spirit, a race of ingenious children who do not want to come of age. This is the Never-Never Land of the 1950s.

Is it purely nostalgia for the past that makes me disturbed by the present? Were courage, aspiration and independence really more in evidence during the twenties and thirties than they are today? I suspect that they were.

We were silly then in many ways: profligate, extreme, impulsive, foolhardy. The harvest of penalties for these faults is still being reaped. But we were also filled with the excitement of apparently limitless horizons. We were eager to battle with odds, take up cudgels, proclaim ideals, achieve excellence, court involvement. We gloried, I may add, in singleness: in being one and not of a group, for difference was a pride. I cannot imagine the concept of Togetherness surviving in that society of aggressive individualism.

Many things certainly are better today than they were then: the mechanics of comfort, eating habits, decoration, hygiene, are some of them. It is possible too that young people are less selfish than we were in the sense that they concern themselves with the community while we were wrapped in our own private glories or grief, oblivious of our neighbors.

Yet it seems to me that they want a house full of things while we wanted a life full of challenge. We wanted change, not stability. Adventure, not security. Difference, not sameness. Risk, not safety. Above all, we were free to think, talk, write, expound and examine any idea in the world, however preposterous or disquieting. And this, more than anything else, is what has been lost in the last decade: this freedom, the reason for our national being. It is grotesque and pitiable that so many of us are still unwilling to say some things out loud.

Who can express doubts about capitalism without being labeled a socialist?

Who can query the concept of God without being called an atheist?

Who can question the virtues of our high standard of living without courting contempt?

Only those speak out who are prepared to accept the suspicion or the rejection such attitudes might bring. Only those who are willing to stand up against the manifold pressures of church, state, commerce, or press for one purpose only: to maintain the status of a free American, right or wrong. It is something a great many seem perfectly willing to lose.

The purpose of this book is to take off some of the gags: to let air in and out; to help pierce this layer of complacency and complaisance. For I think it is only a layer— partly the fatty tissue of prosperity, partly a surface sprayed on by those great appliers of attitudes, the people who sell. I think, in fact, that we have been sold, without our always knowing it, a pretty large bill of goods for which we pay much too dearly. I also think that there are plenty of people in the United States ready to rebel against this bill if it were spelled out clearly enough. It is a wonderful thing to exercise the voice of dissent and the muscles of rebellion. This I propose to do now.

My anger, let it be clear, is one of indignation, not of bitterness. There is a great difference. For bitterness is the reaction to personal hurt, a revenge against suffering. I speak out of a full life, and my anger is directed against the sappers of this fullness in others. The more you believe in human beings, the less can you tolerate the waste of their capacities. The ultimate cynicism is to suspend judgment so that you are not judged. Everything goes. This is the easy way, the pleasant way, the popular way: to abandon standards. And although the ministers and educators of this country intone about "moral and spiritual forces," deploring their obvious decline, the enormous material forces of the country are happily abetting this decline. Prosperity has grown a fatty tissue around conscience. Religion has become not a hair shirt but a contour chair, adjustable to the spirit. Certain words are too troublesome for us now: sacrifice, nobility, courage. Only suckers give up something they want for something others need. Only suckers act purely from moral conviction. Only suckers stick their necks out for what they believe, when what they believe makes others uncomfortable. This is the cynicism of Play It Safe. And it is about as far from the origins of American strength as anything could be. It is, moreover, the matrix of a host of fears which have fastened on us Americans like leeches, sucking out our independence and weakening our will. The effort of living up to ourselves is too great; even our leaders no longer expect it of us, or, for that matter, of themselves. Did I say "leader"? This too is a rejected word, for to lead means to direct and to exact, and no man dare do either. He might be unpopular. What authority we are given now is a trinity: the grin, the generality, and God (the word). These are supposed to guide us to our destiny which has always been assumed to be glorious. No man of power has yet had the courage to tell us that it might be quite the reverse.

If I am angry at much of what we do and think and believe today, it is not because I have a low opinion of Americans but a high opinion of what we could be. Of all the peoples in the world we should be the finest, the freest, the strongest and the bravest. We have been given every chance to be all of these. And because I feel we should be, I refuse to be content, as so many are, with our existent virtues. They are not enough to bring us greatness. They are not even enough, at this point, to ensure our survival.

You will find in this book, therefore, some painful examinations, some impudent swipes, and some harsh indictments. They will not provide solutions but they may stimulate the sluggish circulation. And if they fall into three major and separate categories, which are roughly social, political and personal, it is because of order rather than difference, for each area impinges on, and affects, the other; and each in turn is a reflection of a national and a personal image. The "I" and "We" in these pages are inextricable.

I
THE WAY WE ARE:
THE RITUALS OF EQUALITY

I'M AS GOOD AS YOU ARE

It may be my German blood that makes it possible for me to accept both authority and discipline, and as an American I would worry about this tendency if the rebellious Pole and the questioning Jew were not there to balance and modify it. I share the horror of the world at what this German acceptance has done to it.

Yet our abhorrence of authority and impatience with discipline have, I think, passed the bounds of reason. What they have contributed to our freedom they now contribute to our softness: that spurious and flattening "equality" in which no man is better than his neighbor, in which superiority is denied and leadership is suspect. It is strange that we should distrust strength and leadership when the finest chapters of our history were made by men who exerted authority without tyranny, strength without autocracy, and leadership without the transgression of a single man's rights. But our reaction to the tyrannies of the old world still persists as an obsession. The nature of the American is to resist authority because he believes it to be automatically dangerous and undemocratic. The hero is still the private who shows up the general, the boy who fools his professor, the hoodlum who tricks the police. Freedom has come to mean freedom from authority; a condition we have been enjoying for the past decades at the enormous expense of our strength.

For far longer than that, however, we have come to equate service with servility and respect—unless it is for success, money, or athletic prowess—with a form of obsequiousness. To serve an individual or to serve a state is to be soft-headed. Did not ex-Secretary of Defense Wilson say he was not "smart" to have taken the job in Government? In a democracy you serve yourself.

All this makes for an amorphous and graceless society in which children do not rise when elders enter, in which teachers are bullied, and in which salesgirls, in answer to a query, say "No"—Not "No, sir," or "No, ma'am." It is a society in which bus drivers insult passengers, in which workers can get a full day's pay for a half-day's effort, in which stenographers do not learn to spell. Why should they? Who has the right to demand these things of them? Who is better than they?

I would say: a lot of people, among them those who pay for their services. The individual who employs me is entitled to my deference and courtesy, if not invariably to my respect. So is the colleague with a higher rank and a more responsible position. I believe that age in itself demands deference, and the sight of an old woman standing in a crowded bus while a young person sits shocks me. So does the daily jar of small brutalities: the swingdoor swung in the face, the shoving for place, the insistent horn, the contemptuous telephone voice: "Who do you want?" "What's your number?" "He's not here." Why is the use of those small pleasant words, "Please"; "I'm sorry"; "excuse me"; "thank you," such a burden on our people? Why should respect and courtesy be incompatible with democratic behavior, any more than incivility mark a man as equal to his fellows?

Yet there is the fallacy of equality again. In our society to admit inferiority is to be a fool, and to admit superiority is to be an outcast. Those who are in reality superior in intelligence can be accepted by their fellows only if they pretend they are not. The country is full of poets talking tough, ministers talking homey, and professors talking—well—no better than their students. The more slipshod and colloquial the language, the more regional (preferably the Middle West) the inflection, the more regular the guy. Woe betide the man or woman who speaks with a regard for diction and definition. They sound "superior." And double woe to the man or woman who delights in speech as against talk. A candidate for office can have no greater advantage than muddled syntax; no greater liability than a command of language. As for wit and satire, the weapons of intelligence, their presence in speech constitutes a warning against the speaker, who is presumed by the public to be frivolous, antisocial, untrustworthy—and un-American; in short, unadmirable.

Yet I, for one, would be grossly dishonest if I did not concede and admire in others intelligence or beauty or character superior to my own, and just as dishonest if I denied that certain individuals were less intelligent and less perceptive than myself. The first concession is no more diminishing than the second is inflating. These are facts.

But this whole question of homage and respect is suffused with emotion, and we have been taught that to pay them is somehow debasing, just as domestic service is presumed to debase the one who performs it. "Services" are the pride of our civilization, but "service" and "servant" are bad words. As for taking pride in good service, that is unthinkable. You do what you are paid for, and there is a far greater stigma applied for doing more (sucker is the word) than for doing less.

I remember being dismayed as a student at the girls who faked their homework and took pride in it. Not only were the cheaters not ostracized for cheating: they were usually the most popular girls. Conversely, the diligent students who felt obligations to their teachers were the saps. To have a passion for excellence was to be, at the least, eccentric. And although I realized that this passion led to isolation and loneliness, it took me a very long while to find out that the sure road to acceptance was to get by with the least possible effort.

Perhaps Sputnik has changed this formula, in schools as well as in life. Certainly there will always be, as there have always been, employees who perform more than their expected service to their employers, and students who are dedicated to the excitement of learning. But I suspect that they are in a minority, and that to belong to the majority you must accept the ultimate cynicism: take it easy, you'll get by. Nobody's better than you.

SMILE, SMILE, SMILE

We are, as everyone knows, a very friendly people. Even the Russians concede this. Foreign visitors are overwhelmed with our kindliness and informality, and even Americans returning from abroad feel a wave of warmth rushing out from the continent to greet them. The hearty welcome, the easy smile are among our most endearing traits. But they can be overdone.

The Rheingold Girls smile too much, people in television commercials smile too much, families in magazine ads smile too much, and government leaders smile too much. The American flag is one large grin. Everyone wants to be liked.

This obsessive need to be liked, rather than respected, has become the soft core of our state and our state of mind; as common to the White House as it is to a Coca-Cola ad. In a society of selling you cannot afford to offend the customers. You must try, therefore, to please all.

So this friendliness, this American quality to be cherished, has now been packaged into a product trademarked with a smile and claiming three ingredients: prosperity, piety, and equality. An American who can make money, invoke God, and be no better than his neighbor, has nothing to fear but truth itself. It is better to be liked than brave or free.

There are times, of course, when gravity is not only permissible but required. The stern face may be worn when God is mentioned and the stock market falls; when dignity is assaulted, honesty is impugned, and other nations chastised. Otherwise our teeth, which owe their whiteness and regularity to American dentistry, are to be bared whenever possible as a sign of the good nature for which we are justly famous.

Yet it is doubtful whether Washington or Jefferson or Lincoln ever had to prove their humanity in this manner, and it is difficult to visualize their faces split by a chronic grin. Our greatest president had a profoundly sad face: even his smile must have wrenched the beholder's heart.

But now good-fellowship, unflagging, is the prime requisite for success in our society, and the man or woman who smiles only for reasons of humor or pleasure is a deviate: a prey—and therefore antisocial—to sinister forces. The passport photographer says: "How about a little smile?" The lover, seeing a grave face, says "What's wrong?" A President unsmiling means bad news. To be serious is not to be loved, and that is unbearable.

Now there is clearly nothing wrong with a smile. It can illumine and often make beautiful features dimmed by passivity or grooved by sadness. But the smile I am speaking of, and which so many wear so much, is less an expression of joy than the muscular reflex of popularity. No better, or more horrible, example of this exists than the smile of television masters of ceremonies or the sellers of products: a smile directed at all and therefore at no one, a mass ingratiation wholly devoid of feeling. This kind of promiscuity—for it is exactly that—robs a man both of his dignity and his virility. Poets, dreamers, lovers, fighters and saints—the men who conquer the imagination either through the power of their spirit or the force of their sex have features more often composed by inner disciplines than fragmented by easy grins. They are not popular here.

TWO TYRANNIES

In earlier pages I wrote of a "host of fears which have fastened on us Americans like leeches, sucking out our independence," and also of a "surface sprayed on us by those great appliers of attitudes, the people who sell."

Since women are the buyers of the nation, they in particular have been the victims of two fears which pervade their life and dictate their days: of weight and of age. At the risk of seriously impairing our economy, I herewith propose to relieve them of both obsessions.

"Haven't you lost weight, dear?"

If American men are obsessed with money, American women are obsessed with weight. The men talk of gain, the women talk of loss, and I do not know which talk is the more boring. Certainly both obsessions confine the human being to measurements, the one in digits and the other in inches: wholly material confinements devised to stifle the trapped spirit.

The first thing a woman looks at in another woman these days in her waistline. The first salutation is "You're a little thinner, aren't you?" Or, "Haven't you been putting on a little weight, dear?" The first is the ultimate compliment, the second the ultimate insult. I consider both bad taste, since they are no business of the speaker's. A woman's shape and size is entirely her affair, and if she is happy and hippy she should be left alone. Some of art's greatest nudes have been fleshy, wide and beautiful, and I am willing to wager that their radiance was the reflection of masculine appreciation. It is only fairly recently that men are supposed to prefer the bony splendors of the pelvic cradle.

I am not, let me hasten to say, defending obesity, grossness or flabbiness, for none of these are either healthy or beautiful. Nor am I doubting the beauty of a slim young body. I do very much take issue, however, with the prevailing conviction that there is only one acceptable feminine outline for all ages of her life which—if you except the grotesque mammalian exaggerations of certain film stars—is basically rectilinear, as in a pipe; and that no beauty of face, excitement of mind, or warmth of spirit can excuse or nullify the sin of a widened posterior.

So deep is this conviction, so great the pressures brought to bear on women to maintain it that a great deal of their money and their time goes into a frantic and unremitting struggle against inches. The result is apparent: a race of women far thinner than their mothers at their age and considerably younger in appearance up to the face. There you see the price paid in tension, harassment and preoccupation. There is nothing relaxing about this kind of fight.

There is, of course, a giant conspiracy behind it, for it is the only means by which the corset and girdle industry and the dress industry can continue to profit. There are ways in which a full figure can be beautifully clothed—centuries of design have shown this to be so—but these are not the ways of mass production which depends on the simplest cut and the least fabric. This, in turn, can be worn only by the thin. So that it has become impossible for the woman who is not rich to dress properly if she does not fall within the dimensions of a slender girl of sixteen.

If she cannot force herself within these, she is lost to fashion. Any woman familiar with the clothes produced in what is known as "larger" sizes knows what this means.

They are the shrouds of sex, the sacraments of abdication. If you have to get into these, they seem to say, you might as well give up; *we* have.

Now this is nonsense. There is no reason on earth why a woman who is heavier or broader than this adolescent "ideal" cannot be dressed both fashionably and seductively. Designers and dress manufacturers could see to this if they wanted to. But not only would it demand more material and cut down profit; it would militate against the foundation makers and slenderizing salons and pill-producers of the nation. For then a woman could be attractive without their help, and that would never do.

No, by heaven, whittle her down to size. Their size. And devil take her pocketbook and her peace of mind. Willingly across the nation she sacrifices both for the infinitely dear reward of hearing a woman friend say, "Haven't you lost a little weight, dear?" although the phrase clearly implies that the last time she saw you you were obese.

For this dubious praise she sacrifices too one of the greatest pleasures of life, the eating of good food. To anyone who appreciates this delight, the sight of a woman declining a fine cream sauce, a baked potato, or a crème brulée is more displeasing than admirable. It is also insulting to the cook. I am quite sure, what is more, that a man's pleasure in asking a woman to dinner is considerably diminished by this kind of self-serving abstinence. He might, if given the chance, settle for a few more pounds and a little more gusto. Unless, of course, he is the kind of man—and there are some—who prefer mannequins to women; in which case he isn't worth bothering about in the first place.

So relax, you women tyrannized by tape measures and scales. Have fun, eat well, and be kind to your fellows. And next time a woman remarks on your weight, tell her what she can do with it.

Stay young

Like all people in the middle span, I am aware of death and saddened by its advance forces of disintegration. I do not like the signs in flesh and muscle and bone of slow decline, even if they are yet unaccompanied by pain. To one in love with physical beauty, its inevitable blurring by years is a source of melancholy.

Yet I feel sure that while the flesh may retreat before age, the man or woman can advance if he goes towards death rather than away from it, if he understands the excitement implicit in this progression from the part to the whole. For that is, really, what it should be: a steady ascent from personal involvement—the paths and rocks and valleys and rises of the foothills—to the ultimate height where they fuse into one grand and complex pattern, remote and yet rewarding. It is like coming into clearer air. And if that air becomes in course too rare to breathe, the final breath is one of total purity.

It is because of these convictions that I protest against the American tyranny of youth. There is beauty and freshness in youth (if there is less and less innocence), but it is an accident of time and therefore ephemeral.

There is no "trick" in being young: it happens to you. But the process of maturing is an art to be learned, an effort to be sustained. By the age of fifty you have made yourself what you are, and if it is good, it is better than your youth. If it is bad, it is not because you are older but because you have not grown.

Yet all this is obscured, daily, hourly, by the selling barrage of youth; perhaps the greatest campaign for the arrested development of the human being ever waged anywhere. Look young, be young, stay young, they call from every page and on every air wave. You must be young to be loved. And with this mandate, this threat, this pressure, millions of goods are sold and millions of hours are spent in pursuit of a youth which no longer exists and which cannot be recaptured.

The result of this effort is, in women, obscene; in men, pathetic. For the American woman of middle age thinks of youth only in terms of appearance and the American man of middle age thinks of youth only in terms of virility.

If obscene seems a strong word to use for old women who try to look young, I will be more explicit. It is quite true and quite proper that better eating habits, better care and less drudgery have made American women look ten years younger than their mothers did at the same age. One of the pleasing phenomena of our life is the naturally young and pretty grandmother, almost as lithe and active as her daughter. But I am talking of the still older woman, past her middle fifties, often alone, often idle, who has the means to spend the greater part of her leisure in beauty salons and shops and weight-reducing parlors, resisting age with desperate intensity. They do not know it, but the fact of this resistance nullifies the effects of the effort. The streets of American cities are full of these thin, massaged, made-up, corseted, tinted, overdressed women with faces that are repellent masks of frustration; hard, empty, avid. Although their ankles are slender and their feet perched on backless high-heeled slippers, they fool no one, and certainly no man. They are old legs and old feet. Although their flesh is clear and fairly firm in the visible areas, it is kneaded flesh, and fools no one. The hips are small indeed, but the girdle only emphasizes their stiff aridity. And the uplift bra, the platinum hair, the tight dress? Whom do they fool? The woman herself, alone. And the obscenity in all this is that she uses the outward techniques of sexual allure to maintain her youth when she is no longer wanted by men. And she does it because she has been told to do it by the advertising media. She has been sold a bill of goods.

Let me hastily say at this point that it is the solemn duty of all women to look as well as they can and to maintain through life the grooming that makes them pleasing to others. Towards this end, the advertisers have performed a signal service to Americans. But they have over-reached themselves, and us. Instead of saying "Be yourself," they say, "Be Young." Instead of saying "Relax," they say "Compete!" In doing this, they deprive the maturing woman of a great joy, an astounding relief: the end, not of sex, heaven knows, but of sexual competition. By the time a woman is fifty she is either wanted as a woman of fifty or not really wanted at all. She does not have to fool her husband or her lover, and she knows that competition with women far younger than she is not only degrading but futile.

It is also an axiom that the more time a woman spends on herself, the less she has for others and the less desirable she is to others. If this goes for young women—and I

believe it does—it goes doubly for older women, who have
—if they knew it—more to give.

When I go to Europe and see the old people in villages
in France or Italy, for instance, I am struck at once by the
age of all women who are no longer young, pitying their
premature withering; and at the same time startled by the
occasional beauty of their old faces. Lined and grooved
and puckered as they may be, their hair grizzled or lank,
there is something in their eyes and in their bones that
gives age austerity and makes their glossy contemporaries
at a bridge table here seem parodies of women. They
show that they have lived and they have not yet found
the means to hide it.

I remember also that as a child and a young girl I
never thought of my mother in terms of age. Whatever it
was at any time, she looked it; and nobody then told her
to lose weight or do something about her hair because she
was far too interesting a human being to need such
"ameliorations." It would, indeed, have been an imperti-
nence. My mother had no illusions of beauty: she was too
concerned with music and her husband and her children
to be concerned, in detail, with herself. I don't doubt
that, given today's aids, she could have looked younger
and smarter than she did. But she would have lost something. The time and effort spent in improving her looks
would have been taken from music and from love. With
her unruly eyebrows plucked to a thin line, her face
made-up, her plump, small body moulded into girdles,
an important part of her would have vanished: her identity.

It is this that the older women of America are losing.
At club gatherings, at hotels, at resorts, they look identi-
cal. What lives they have led have been erased from their

faces along with the more obvious marks of age. They have smoothed and hardened into a mould. Their lotions have done well.

It could be said that if they maintain the illusion of youth to themselves only, no harm is done and some good. But I wonder if all self-deceptions do not harm, and if their price is not loss of self.

I wonder too whether one of the reasons for wild, intemperate, destructive youth might not be this same hard finish, this self-absorption, of the women to whom they might otherwise turn. I cannot imagine going for counsel and comfort to a mother or aunt or grandmother tightly buttressed by lastex and heavily masked by make-up. Where is the soft wide lap, the old kind hands, the tender face of age?

None of us with any pride in person and any sense of aesthetics can allow ourselves to crumble into decay without trying to slow the process or at least veil its inroads. But that is not the major battle. The fight is not for what is gone but for what is coming; and for this the fortification of the spirit is paramount, the preservation of the flesh a trivial second.

Let the queen bee keep her royal jelly. Or so I keep telling myself.

4

THE HALF-PEOPLE

People on horses look better than they are. People in cars look worse than they are. On any of our highways this last observation, unfortunate as it may be, is inescapable. For the car, by bisecting the human outline, diminishes it, producing a race of half-people in a motion not of their own making.

Automobiles can be handsome things, particularly if they are foreign, but they bestow none of their power and beauty on their passengers. It is not only that the people in them face in one direction, like gulls in a wind or curious penguins, but that the sleekness and brightness of the cars' exterior makes them look shabby if not downright sordid. It also in some mysterious way accentuates the baser characteristics. Boys under twenty in cars look delinquent; men over thirty shifty and gross. Most middle-aged women look bad-tempered, and most young women hard. Children in cars are either asleep or unmanageable, jumping up and down in the back seat, leaning over the front seat, or pressing dirty faces against the rear window. Only dogs, I think, preserve their charm; there is nothing more attractive than the canine face shoved out of the window inhaling the sharp breeze and the myriad smells it carries.

Cars do something sinister to the relationship of the sexes. I do not know what is more disturbing: the husband and wife in the front seat facing forward, speechless, with set mouths, as if their destination were doomed and their communications broken; or the young couple intertwined and two-headed, the delinquent driving with one hand and half a mind. On a bench their closeness would be endearing; on a highway it is alarming.

Cars have bestowed motion but removed dignity. And if they have given us one sort of freedom, they have become also small prisons, in which a group of people are locked within steel walls, motionless in movement, changeless during change, and borne inexorably in a direction which is not always of their choosing.

Get a horse.

5

WASTELAND

Cans. Beer cans. Glinting on the verges of a million miles of roadways, lying in scrub, grass, dirt, leaves, sand, mud, but never hidden. Piels, Rheingold, Ballantine, Schaefer, Schlitz, shining in the sun or picked by moon or the beams of headlights at night; washed by rain or flattened by wheels, but never dulled, never buried, never destroyed. Here is the mark of savages, the testament of wasters, the stain of prosperity.

Who are these men who defile the grassy borders of our roads and lanes, who pollute our ponds, who spoil the purity of our ocean beaches with the empty vessels of their thirst? Who are the men who make these vessels in millions and then say, "Drink—and discard"? What society is this that can afford to cast away a million tons of metal and to make of wild and fruitful land a garbage heap?

What manner of men and women need thirty feet of steel and two hundred horsepower to take them, singly, to their small destinations? Who demand that what they eat is wrapped so that forests are cut down to make the paper that is thrown away, and what they smoke and chew is sealed so that the sealers can be tossed in gutters and caught in twigs and grass?

What kind of men can afford to make the streets of their towns and cities hideous with neon at night, and their roadways hideous with signs by day, wasting beauty; who leave the carcasses of cars to rot in heaps; who spill their trash into ravines and make smoking mountains of refuse for the town's rats? What manner of men choke off the life in rivers, streams and lakes with the waste of their produce, making poison of water?

Who is as rich as that? Slowly the wasters and despoilers are impoverishing our land, our nature, and our beauty, so that there will not be one beach, one hill, one lane, one meadow, one forest free from the debris of man and the stigma of his improvidence.

Who is so rich that he can squander forever the wealth of earth and water for the trivial needs of vanity or the compulsive demands of greed; or so prosperous in land that he can sacrifice nature for unnatural desires? The earth we abuse and the living things we kill will, in the end, take their revenge; for in exploiting their presence we are diminishing our future.

And what will we leave behind us when we are long dead? Temples? Amphora? Sunken treasure?

Or mountains of twisted, rusted steel, canyons of plastic containers, and a million miles of shores garlanded, not with the lovely wrack of the sea, but with the cans and bottles and light-bulbs and boxes of a people who conserved their convenience at the expense of their heritage, and whose ephemeral prosperity was built on waste.

6

KEEP OUT THE AIR

Look at any window in any house in any town in the United States, and what do you see? The half-lowered shade or blind. It does not matter if the window faces north or south, if it is a bright day or a dark day, if it is morning or afternoon; it does not matter if the window looks on trees or hills or the next house; half of the window's light is barred by blinds. Why? So that the sun will not fade the fabrics? Today's fabrics do not fade, and besides, the sun never enters half of these windows. Privacy? The lower half of the window is unshielded, and in any case what do a wholly gregarious people want with privacy? Appearances? What is handsome in a window half obscured by yellow shade or white slats? Gentility? Whose gentility? And why is it genteel to admit only half the available light?

This half-shade, you can plainly see, has become an obsession; unconscious in the nation, conscious in me. I do not know the reason for it, but I think I see a meaning in it. It is a fear of exposure in the deepest sense. Three hundred years ago it may have been as simple as a fear of the outer wilderness; a need to shutter out the dangerous night and shutter in the small close world of man. I can understand the shade drawn wholly against the unknown. But why half against the known?

Strangely, I think the half-drawn blind is still part of a general fear of the elements, and in particular of light and air. It is also part of our muffled state, shared by the body as well as the mind. In diminishing the effects of weather we have diminished our resistance to it, and it is a matter of constant amazement to me that the nation's health authorities do not see the price we pay for our protections: against cold and heat, against wind and rain; against the natural efforts and adjustments of the body.

In winter the heat in most houses, offices, shops, schools, public places and public carriers is far beyond what is needed for comfort and indicated for health. A greater part of our people live without air all day long, and muffle their children up to the ears in airtight clothes at the first hint of cold. Women in fur coats shop in stores too hot for salesgirls in silks. On the first crisp days, no windows in the superheated buses are opened, although the passengers are dressed for outside weather. The fear of cold leaves the park empty on days when sun and wind make it beautiful; days when a park in Europe is full of children playing and people walking. And rain? Who walks in rain except to the nearest shelter? Who, in fact, walks—except foreigners and faddists?

Americans are so protected by the marvels of their technology that their bundled children succumb to every bug, their adolescent boys have night-club pallor and smoker's chests (the girls do better: vanity saves them), and men and women suffer the chronic twin fatigues of annoxia and inertia: a life without air and without movement. Is it then any wonder that telephone linemen, oil drillers, cow-hands and forest rangers are the best-looking men in the land?

The only way to restore some degree of vigor in the American body would be in the construction of communities where the men would walk to work and the children to school. Where boys would not be permitted the use of automobiles until they were twenty. Where health authorities would regulate the temperature of public places to a level best for public health. Where every able-bodied citizen, young and old, would have a mandatory period daily of exposure to whatever weather existed, however bad. I would also like to see one day a week when all facilities were suspended: light, heat, gas and water. We might then learn an independence which could teach us ultimate survival. Rigor is a good governess.

When nature is overridden, she takes her revenge. Though science has lengthened our span, it may have weakened our fiber; and if nature cannot harm us, neither can she endow us now with her strength. We have put up all sorts of shields against her reality, and the half-drawn shade is one of them. One more evasion of truth: a word which, in our present vocabulary, is synonymous with discomfort. So we temper the brilliance of light and the sting of air, stewing in our own juice.

7

THE PATIO AND THE PRIVATE LIFE

If we lower the blind on our windows, we pull up the shades on our lives. Americans now delight in two forms of exposure. In Togetherness, families are continually exposed to each other and to their neighbors, privacy implying a sense of superiority which none may claim. In books and television interviews, individuals bare their souls to the multitudes with every evidence of relish.

I submit the following sketch as being fairly typical of the kind of volume ghost-written by women who have lain down the easy way and come up the hard way, landing—almost invariably—on the best-seller lists.

Gutter Girl, or *I Made My Bed*

The cards were stacked. When my grandmother, a wealthy North Shore dowager, saw me two days after I was born, she said, "In China, they would drown her."

At that time my father, the operatic idol of seven capitals, was already drinking heavily. At my christening he forced champagne down my tiny throat. When I hiccuped he roared, "That's my girl! I'll make a bum of you yet!" My mother, white-lipped, left the house. I did not see her again for ten years.

During that time, I lived with my father, Ricardo Neri, the greatest Siegfried of his time and, some say, of all time. Born Dick Black, his magnificent physique, his Greek features, and his tireless lungs had made him the brightest star in the Metropolitan's firmament.

His appetite for women was inexhaustible. In his enormous house, which was modeled after Valhalla, women came and went. I called them all Mummy and they taught me many things. At five there was nothing I did not know.

"My little one," said father, "you too will be a great singer, and to be a great singer, you must have lived." He saw to it that I did.

He had constructed one great hall of his house to give

the illusion, with layers of green and blue scrim and a few giant water plants of papier mâché, of the Rhine River, and had installed all the complicated apparatus necessary for his "Rhine Maidens" to "float" through the "water." In his drinking bouts it used to amuse him to attach his various lights of love to pulleys and send them screaming through the Rhine.

I was a lonely child; old before my time. I worshiped my father and he worshiped me. His one ambition was that I should follow in his footsteps, and when I was fifteen he persuaded the Metropolitan that I was ready to sing *Carmen*.

I will never forget my debut. There I was, Rita Neri, daughter of the great Ricardo Neri, facing the Diamond Horseshoe. When I came out of the cigarette factory, swinging my hips, the ovation was thunderous. "Bravo! Bravo!" they cried. I had to sing to stop from choking.

I do not know how I got through my ordeal. I was in another world, sustained only by the thought that I was a Neri. I remember that in the middle of the "Habanera" someone next to me hissed, "B-flat—not A!" But I was used to jealousy.

After it was all over, my father crushed me tenderly in his great arms. There were tears in his eyes. "You were . . ." he said, but could not go on.

Even my mother came to the green room, in sables. "My little Poopsie!" she cried, "With a rose in her teeth!"

The Director of the Metropolitan looked at me gravely and said, "I have never seen such a Carmen." It was a night of triumph.

But it was too soon. I was not ready for it. I wanted love. I wanted oblivion. That night I found both in the

eyes of a glorious young waiter. We went off after the
party, away from all the glitter, to his room in Delancey
Street. Every night he beat me unconscious and every day
we made up. But a week later he left me for a catering
job. All he said as he left was, "It won't work."

I stumbled from bar to bar, drinking Gibsons. People
looked at me strangely. In one bar I met a man I used to
know and he got me a job in a night club. Singing dirty
songs. With my red eyes and matted hair, I reminded
people of an existentialist chanteuse. I didn't care.

One night I met a poet with gentle eyes. He took me to
his room in a flophouse and read to me. We had no money
and no food, but we had something else. Every night Paul
would go to the basement and get the cheese out of the
rat trap before the rat did, and with what was left in the
bottom of discarded beer cans we made festive little din-
ners.

I remembered an exclusive restaurant where my father
used to take me, and once a week I would go to the back
door at ten at night and ask Gaston for leftovers. On my
sixteenth birthday he gave me half a duck-bigarade, a
quarter strawberry tart, and a third of a bottle of St. Emi-
lion. I hurried back to the flophouse. Paul had left a note.
"There is no future in this," it said.

I gave the duck to the rat and stumbled blindly into the
street. A one-way street. It had been a one-way street
since I was born.

When I was seventeen I looked thirty-five. When I was
eighteen I looked forty-six. When I was nineteen . . . In
my twentieth year, after five hundred men and a thousand
Gibsons, both my parents came to a violent end. My beautiful mother was charged by a rhinoceros on safari, and a
week later my father was found dead at the bottom of his

Rhine, tangled in harness. It must have been a practical joke.

Half-conscious, stumbling through the gay, heedless crowds in the bright sun of upper Fifth Avenue, I heard a voice.

"Rita! Poopsie Neri!" Pushing my hair away from my dark glasses, I strained to see. Somehow, through the fog of degradation, I managed to recognize an old lover of my mother's—a publisher.

"What do you want of me?" I muttered thickly.

"A book," he said, as he guided me to his office. "And don't leave out a single thing!"

I didn't.

The other form of exposure is, as I have said, Togetherness: a term devised by a national magazine with the avowed purpose of strengthening family ties and the more immediately practical purpose of increasing consumer buying by appealing not to Mom alone but to Dad and Junior and Sis too.

So popular has this concept become in all the mass media, and so faint the line between moral purpose and product promotion, that the following sketch could not resist being written.

Miltown Place, or *Life With Sponsors*

My family couldn't brush their teeth after every meal, but we had something more precious together. I guess you could call it "togetherness."

My mother and father did everything together, and so did we. I can't remember a single moment when there wasn't a family-size bottle of Coke on the indoor barbecue pit.

So many scenes flash through my mind as I think of those years in Crestwood: my father, laughing through his smoke rings as he chortled, "Winston tastes good!"; Aunt Birdie, who came from Mobile, chirping roguishly "Lahk a cigarette should!"; my mother seeing my teen-age sister Shirley off to a dance with the heart-warming whisper: "Don't be half-safe!"

My mother was the most unforgettable character I had ever met. I see her now, rubbing her freshly ironed wash against her cheek and murmuring of its whiteness; or rushing to my father as he came home from work and crying, "Darling, have you heard the wonderful news?" Professional laundries use *soap,* not detergents!" My mother had that kind of mind.

We children spent many childhood hours browsing through old *Reader's Digests*. "It's the small things that count," my father always used to say. Years later, in the isolation booths of jackpot shows, we used to thank our stars for the rich background of knowledge those little old *Digests* gave us. Everyone said we sparkled.

Every Sunday we had Norman Vincent Peale for dinner, and Mother used to make Kraft pizzas for him. He often remarked on her sealed-in goodness and creamy richness. Some people said it was Geritol, but we knew that it was her moral and spiritual values that made her like that.

"Never forget," she used to say when she sipped her calorie-free beer. "This is a friendly, freedom-loving nation."

The only sad note in those unforgettable years concerned my nearest brother, Prelvis. He lived in a dream world of his own. "I wonder," he would say, vacantly, "where the yellow went!" But he had great sweetness in him, and my mother was infinitely patient. Even when he ice-skated over the kitchen floor, she would merely run a mop over the wax and the tracks would disappear. "No rub, no wipe!" she would quip merrily as she rubbed and wiped.

The most unforgettable character I ever knew (next to Mother) was our family doctor, whom we called "Doc." Whenever any of us were sick, no matter what from, "Doc" would draw little pictures of our intestines and show us how fast Bufferin brought relief. (He was the fifth out of four doctors.)

Yet we were not without romance. I will never forget when Shirley married Bob and he gave her a set of flat silver. As she looked up into his eyes, fingering a salad fork, he said, with infinite tenderness, "This Regency pattern is another way of saying 'I love you.'" Putting on my Playtex "living gloves" to help Mother with the dishes, I yearned for a love like that. "With Joy," she comforted me, instinctively, "dishwashing is *almost* nice!"

Part of our "togetherness" in those days was the sharing of minds as well as hands, and, of course, the spirit. Each of us prayed before our respective tasks: Father before his board meeting, Mother before cooking, us children before exams. Every morning Mother read aloud from Mr. Peale's column in *Look*, and once a week Father read us the *Life* editorial, to set us straight. And on Christmas Eve, we joined our voices to Bing Crosby's as he sang carols from Hollywood.

I will never forget when our world fell apart. It was the year when four out of five doctors said "Anxiety is Good for You." This marked the end of an era.

My mother no longer rubs her cheek against her wash or lets something golden happen with Fluffo. She plays a bull fiddle and reads Ionescu.

My father wears hair shirts and corresponds with Françoise Sagan; my sister Shirley and Bob got divorced after she put his Ike buttons in the Disposall, and Prelvis is waiting for Godot in a degraded Southern town.

Miltown Place, the Temple of Togetherness, has been sold to the Society for the Propagation of the Failure.

And I? As I write, I am lying in a stupor from Wolfschmidt, sucking my thumb.

II
POLITICS AND PREJUDICES

THE VIEWS OF THE SPEAKER DO
NOT NECESSARILY REPRESENT ...

The following is a transcript of an imaginary television interview between a Professional Prober and myself.

PP: Miss Mannes, before I ask you any questions about your political beliefs, I would like to quote from something you have just written. It begins this way:

"This is the story," you wrote, "of a man who woke up one morning and found the dictionary changed. The word "freedom," for instance, was defined as "lack of control"; "liberty" as "freedom from responsibility," and "equality" as "the state of being no better than others." The definition for "progress" was "inertial guidance." But the thing that upset the man most was the definition of the word "liberal." It had the abbreviations for "archaic" and "obsolete" after it and the following comments: "formerly used to describe members of the Democratic, as opposed to the Republican, Party in the United States, and to denote a belief in civil rights, social reform, collective bargaining, international cooperation, and the works of such men as Tom Paine, Bertrand Russell, and Franklin Delano Roosevelt. Also loosely applied to adherents of leftist philosophies and to any American opposed to Senator McCarthy (1952-56). Since 1956, however, the term "liberal" has become a meaningless cliché, applied to Republicans in favor of foreign aid and public housing as well as to Democrats (Southern) who recognize the voting rights of Negroes. It is also used in a general sense to imply a sense of futility, or loss of direction."

Miss Mannes, let me ask you this: Isn't this an admission that liberals are finished?

MM: No. It's merely an admission that the word "liberal" is, as I wrote, obsolete.

PP: But you call yourself a liberal, don't you?

MM: I don't call myself anything. Other people do.

PP: Well, let me follow your imaginary liberal further. You wrote of him here: "His worst fears were now confirmed; he had no name and no direction, and he felt that his passport to action, so heavily stamped during the previous twenty years by excursions into the future, had been taken from him and confiscated by some bland, unseen official in a borderless realm." What did you mean by that?

MM: I mean that there is not much choice between Republicans who adopt Democratic policies and Democrats who believe that the only way a Democratic policy can win is by resembling Republican policy as much as possible. This is a no-man's land, without borders. You cannot move and act in this kind of void. Protest withers in the throat and rage is directionless.

PP: And yet, you have made your choice, have you not? You are a Democrat, aren't you?

MM: I am.

PP: And still in this same piece you say of your liberal that "his annoyance at Republican oratory, Republican faces and Republican salesmanship was not a sufficient

launching pad for flight into space. There were Democratic faces and Democratic evasions that turned his stom-
ach, and even when a Democrat talked well, he said
nothing new." If you really believe that, Miss Mannes,
why are you a Democrat?

MM: I suppose because the Democratic past comes much
nearer to what I believe than the Republican present.

PP: Then the Democrats have no future?

MM: Not until they make one for themselves. But I believe they will.

PP: Before I ask you why, I'd like to go back to *your* past,
and ask you whether you have always been interested in
politics—and why.

MM: I spent my youth supremely indifferent to politics.
All I was interested in was what I called "life," which was
love, and what I called "art," which was theatre and painting and writing and sculpture and talk.

PP: But a lot was happening politically in the late twenties and thirties. Didn't you care?

MM: I didn't because I thought politics had nothing to do
with life. I remember echoes of Sacco and Vanzetti, but I
didn't understand the issues. I remember the crash because people jumped out of windows and suddenly everybody was nicer because nobody had any money.

PP: But didn't that affect you deeply?

MM: No.

PP: Why?

MM: Because my parents were musicians who lived fru-
gally on what they earned, and had no stocks or bonds.
In spite of everything, they went on playing and teaching
and my brother and I went on studying and working, and
nothing changed very much. You see, we knew that money
was necessary to live, but we never liked money. It was a

dirty word. And we hardly knew any rich people then anyway.

PP: But then what *did* finally wake you up—politically, I mean?

MM: Hitler and Roosevelt.

PP: Why do you lump them together? Because they were alike?

MM: Of course not. Because they represented to me at that time—and still do—the forces of darkness and light. When I first read and heard Hitler's speeches I recognized pure evil. When I first listened to Roosevelt, I heard the words I wanted to hear.

PP: What words?

MM: The words an American should use. They were words of sanity and leadership and courage, and for the first time I could say of a man in government, "that man speaks for me."

PP: What made you so sure Roosevelt was right? A great many people considered him as dangerous as Hitler.

MM: I remember them—with contempt. Why did I think he was right? Because I felt that his ultimate direction was the right one.

PP: What do you mean by his ultimate direction?

MM: The general direction of human society; the broadening of the base of government to include—and benefit—most of the people. He released the American potential and he related it to the rest of the world. He was, in fact, a citizen of the world.

PP: Judging from your remarks, Miss Mannes, you must have belonged to that group of idealists in the thirties who believed that socialism and communism were the salvation of the masses and the world. Would you care to comment on that?

MM: I expected that one! Yes, I did believe there were better ways for people to live than our own—at that time —and certain social and economic inequities made me furious. But so, equally, did the dogma of communism and the loose generalities of socialism. I did not see the answer in either of them.

PP: Isn't there some hindsight in that? Aren't you rationalizing—or whitewashing?

MM: My record, and I say this without pride, is clear. I am not now, never have been, and—

PP: (Smiling) All right. Let's get back to FDR a minute. Weren't you ever aware that he antagonized and harmed a great many people?

MM: Antagonized, of course. Any man of real conviction does. As for harm, I find the myth of Roosevelt's "ruin of private enterprise" as preposterous as most of the fables circulated by a hydrophobic press and psychotic political enemies.

PP: Those are strong words. Wouldn't they apply to you as well?

MM: I don't think anger at distortion of fact and at personal spite comes under either of those headings. I think the behavior of professional Roosevelt-haters does. They hate him dead as much as they hated him alive, and those are hardly healthy emotions.

PP: I gather, then, that you have no criticism of FDR at all?

MM: Only fools deny his errors, his vanities, and his occasionally devious methods to achieve certain obvious ends.

PP: How would you describe him, then?

MM: As a great leader, who did his country infinitely more good—in war and in peace—than harm.

PP: So that's why you became a Democrat?

MM: Partly, but not wholly.

PP: What do you mean?

MM: Well, I mean that the more interested I became in how we were governed, the more I began to realize that there was more to politics than the names of parties.

PP: I still don't understand.

MM: What I'm trying to say is that certain kinds of people become Republicans and certain kinds of people become Democrats, and that it's more than a matter of party affiliations. It's a way of thinking and being.

PP: You really mean to say that there's just one way of being a Democrat and one way of being a Republican?

MM: No, unfortunately. They're both split in two, and I don't recognize a man like Eastland or Talmadge as being a true Democrat any more than a true Republican recognized a man like McCarthy as a representative of his party —or, let's say—Goldwater or Jenner now.

PP: What do you mean by a true Republican or a true Democrat?

MM: I guess I mean a person who believes in the fundamental philosophy of his party, the main line; avoiding, in either case, reaction or radicalism. For purposes of this discussion I would like to leave out the lunatic fringe of both parties and stick to the "ideal," or "typical."

PP: All right, I'll go along with you there. What do you consider a typical Republican?

MM: I think, primarily, he is a man with a strong sense of social status, however limited, and a deep allegiance to business, preferably big.

PP: Is there anything wrong with that?

MM: I'm not saying it's wrong or right. I'm merely saying it's what Republicans are like and why I could never be one.

PP: Why couldn't you be one?

MM: Because I don't care for social status and because I don't think business is a primary aim of life. Republicans seem to me to be chiefly concerned with holding on to what they have: in society, it's position, or respectability, or what you will; in business, of course, it's profit.

PP: You don't like respectability?

MM: I don't like people who are conscious of being the "right" people, and whether they're on top or not, Republicans have always considered themselves to be an elite of respectability. To be a Republican is considered to be socially acceptable. It is also, in business, supposed to constitute a seal of integrity.

PP: Are you trying to say that Republicans haven't integrity?

MM: Nothing of the sort. No party has a monopoly on integrity or corruption. My point is that the Republicans *think* they have a corner on morality and the Democrats don't.

PP: But you are saying, aren't you, that Republicans are snobs?

MM: In a sense, yes. But then, so are the Democrats.

PP: Then what's the difference?

MM: The difference is in the nature of the snobbery. The Democrats think they are more intelligent than the Republicans, and I prefer that basis of assumption more than the social or economic one . . . even if it is only an assumption.

PP: But aren't you saying that the Republicans, being an elite, aren't really democratic? That they are above the people, so to speak?

MM: No, I'm not saying exactly that. But I cannot help feeling that when a Republican expresses concern for "the people" or minorities or for the underprivileged, it's an expression of benevolence rather than identification. Naturally, they deny this. But there is no question in my mind as to which party has concerned itself more closely and more continually with the needs of the people.

PP: Then why didn't the people vote for them in the last election?

MM: Because, like all people who are prosperous and fat, they preferred the party of consolidation to the party of change. They wanted a safe thing and what they thought was a safe man.

PP: And didn't they get that?

MM: They got a vacuum.

PP: Which nature abhors?

MM: Which my nature certainly does.

PP: But tell me, Miss Mannes, how do you explain the fact that so many of what they call "the little people" went Republican in 1952?

MM: Apart from a case of hero worship and a campaign that sold them a phony bill of goods, I am sure it was to improve their social and business status. As I said, it was more respectable.

PP: Do you deny that they became Republican out of disgust with Democratic corruption?

MM: The mess in Washington? What do you think is happening there now? If Democrats can be corrupt and venal, so can Republicans. But at least Democrats don't speak of crusades.

PP: What else do you think of as typical Republicans?

MM: Oh, I think they are inclined to be pious and solemn and very unfunny. At least, this administration has been singularly without humor or wit. And if you want to go back to Hoover, or Coolidge, or . . .

PP: Let's stick to the present.

MM: All right. I'll stick to Democrats for a change. It's hardly an accident that nearly every major talent in the United States in the arts or sciences is a Democrat—if not by affiliation then by inclination.

PP: You seem to have forgotten a group called C.A.S.E. in the last election.

MM: Oh yes, the Committee of Arts and Sciences for Eisenhower. I thought it was slightly pathetic.

PP: There were some distinguished names on it.

MM: I don't deny that. But a pitiful few compared to those who were *not* on it . . . and a pitiful attempt of a party long allergic to intellectuals and creative people to lure them to it. No. I don't think it's possible to write a good play or paint a good picture and be a good Republican.

PP: What do you mean by 'good'?

MM: I don't mean successful. I mean truly creative and honest and original.

PP: If this is so, why do you think it is so?

MM: Well, I think the overwhelming majority of people who are engaged in the processes of thought and expression are Democrats because the essence of thought is exploration and diversity and change. It's impossible to have vision in art or government without risk, or the boldness and courage which produce risk. And this—in spite of what they call modern Republicanism—is the antithesis of true Republican thinking.

PP: Do you mean to say that Republicans have no vision?

MM: I mean they have a restricted vision. To be Republican is to equate conservatism with caution; to extend the known present into the unknown future with a minimum of change; to prefer conformity over diversity.

PP: Isn't this wisdom?

MM: I would call it fear.

PP: Let's see if I get this straight. What you're telling me, really, is that the Democrats have a monopoly on courage, vision, and intelligence. And yet you said a while ago that no party can have a monopoly on integrity or corruption. How can you attribute virtues to one set of Americans rather than another?

MM: I am attributing virtues to a way of thinking and not to the individual who thinks them. In other words, I believe that the philosophical and social premises of the Democratic party have more courage and vision and sense than Republican party doctrines.

PP: And therefore we should have a one-party system with a strong man like Roosevelt on top?

MM: Hardly. The two-party system is fine so long as each party stands firmly for what it believes and acts in accordance—

PP: Wouldn't that mean having the Democrats throw out the Dixiecrats, and the Republicans throw out the dinosaurs?

MM: Yes. And Republicans not taking over Democratic platforms and Democrats not talking like Republicans. The hope of the Democrats is to move ahead and think back.

PP: Isn't that a contradiction?

MM: I don't think so. When the Democrats stand still, they lose. When they move forward, they win.

PP: Miss Mannes, can you think of any circumstances in which you would vote for a Republican president?

MM: Yes. If a man like Lincoln were nominated. But that is hardly in the realm of possibility.

PP: Because we can no longer produce great men?

MM: No. Because today a man like Lincoln would not be a Republican.

PP: One more question, Miss Mannes. Have you found that your views have affected your social or professional life in any way?

MM: Socially, yes. For years my few Republican friends considered me un-housebroken, to be kept out of the living room; and the more expedient Democrats were embarrassed by me. In the early fifties, remember, Democrats were dangerous fellows and the President was God.

PP: And professionally?

MM: Well, certainly in the years of McCarthy, people like me had few forums—in print or on the air. An overwhelmingly Republican press is no help either. But things are looking up. After all, here I am—on the air!

PP: And here I am—off it! Thank you for coming tonight.

(*Turns to audience*)

Ladies and gentlemen, you have just been listening to the kind of partisan that makes our democratic society so lively and our elections so stormy. Next week, we will hear from a Republican congresswoman who feels that Outer Space should be Our Space. Good-night until next week!

2

FANTASY: INAUGURAL ADDRESS, 1960

Fellow Americans: As I assume, in pride and humility, this highest office in the land, I can promise you only one thing; and that is honesty. Honesty in facing situations, honesty in dealing with them, and honesty in telling you about them. I will hide nothing from you, including my own doubts as to the right course and my own fears as to the gravity of any given condition. So long as my health, which is now excellent, prevails, I will not delegate the authority or the responsibility of the Chief Executive to anyone, nor will I permit any impingements of it by the legislative branch of government. I am not only the servant of my people but the commander-in-chief of our forces for defense and the final arbiter of our foreign policy. This is determined by our constitution, which I am pledged to uphold.

I will not oppose the opposition party merely for the sake of opposing them, nor will I support members of my own party, who attempt to obstruct our party's policies, merely because they are members. If I cannot persuade the bigoted, the fearful, and the rash towards reason, I would rather risk the loss of their support than the division of our party. We can survive more strongly without the lunatic fringe.

I will pander to no group for the sake of securing its votes, whether that group is economic, racial, national, or religious; although I will listen to all just demands from whatever group and no matter how small a minority of our citizens. But if Labor transgresses its rights I will tell them so in the same manner that I would attempt to control similar greeds or monopolies of Business, and if legislation were necessary to keep either within constructive bounds, I would not hesitate to request it from Congress. The price exacted from the American citizen by the demands both of Labor and of Business have been too high, and the squeeze—potentially dangerous—has already been felt. The average American pays too much for his home, his schools, his food, his health and his security.

As for our major problem of race, I uphold unequivocally the constitutional guarantees for all Americans, Negroes and white, for equal rights and integrated schooling, however difficult and painful this may be to achieve in certain parts of our nation, however long or rough the road. We cannot pretend to be a free society and at the same time maintain these degrading and perilous divisions on the basis of color alone. On the other hand, the mere fact of being a Negro and a member of a minority group, however large, does not endow a man with any superior rights but entails, rather, equal responsibilities: a fact which anger and resentment and frustration, however natural, sometimes obscure. I would say to Negroes then, you must have equal opportunities: but you must make equal contributions to our society too, and that will take superior effort.

As for the major problem of the world at large, which is

the maintenance of peace and the avoidance of holocaust, I have this to say. I believe the testing of thermonuclear weapons to be a crime against humanity which no arguments of relative defensive advantage can rationalize, and I demand that both the testing and making of nuclear armaments be stopped now by international agreements, however crude and tentative these may be initially, and at whatever risk of attempted betrayal by one party to them. The alternative risk is an irresistible progression, through a mounting armaments race, towards total war and total annihilation.

As for the exploration of outer space, no man can stop the human thirst for knowledge or the creative genius which must satisfy it, at whatever expenditure of time and energy. But to know is not to kill: in fact, destruction is the end of knowledge. So let us continue our journey into the universe, along with all other nations. I will only say this, that I still believe the exploration of inner space to be the more important, for until we know what motivates the hearts and minds of men we can understand nothing outside ourselves, nor will we ever reach fulfillment as that greatest miracle of all, the human being.

I will say one more thing, fellow Americans, and it will not please you. Former leaders of yours have told you, in triumph, that you never had it so good. I am going to tell you now that you have had it too good—not in terms of human fulfillment, but in terms of material gain. The pursuit of happiness has become the pursuit of things: and there comes a time when the acquisition of things exacts the loss of self. A rich diet does not make a strong people, and this is what you must be in these years to come, or prepare yourselves for defeat by stronger ones. So I am warning you now that your diet may be reduced and your possessions diminished in order to strip the fat off the nation's bones and restore its muscle. I will propose certain measures which will deprive you of certain luxuries which you do not need for the urgencies which are to be required of us as a nation: the finest education, the greatest skills, the most comprehensive knowledge in all fields . . . and, most important of all, the conscience of Americans, than which nothing on this earth has greater value.

3

HANDBOOK OF SUBVERSION

The following is a memo from the publisher of *The Daily Ruse and Smearer,* New York's greatest tabloid, to a new editorial writer:

Welcome aboard, Ed. I'm glad to have you with us, and I know our four million readers will be too.

You are familiar, I know, with the policies of the Daily Ruse, but I would like to take this opportunity to express to you, as clearly as I can, our basic philosophy concerning the function of this newspaper as a molder and mirror of public opinion. You might regard this as a sort of primer of editorial writing, to be used as a guide and pattern, applicable to any situation or event or personality which you bring to public attention. It may also answer some of the questions which are sure to arise from time to time in the pursuit of your work.

The most important thing of all is to know the people you are talking to—and writing for: the four million inhabitants of the greatest city in the world who buy the Daily Ruse. Do not overestimate them: they are human beings. This means that they are not very intelligent, not very noble, and not very cultured. They are, in fact, semi-literate. They know very few words, so confine yourself to those words and don't use any of more than two syllables except for wholly familiar terms like "patriotism," "loyalty," "motherhood," etc. Above all, keep your sentences short and your paragraphs short. Our readers can retain only one thought at a time, so do not confuse them with several. The act of reading itself is difficult enough for the Daily Ruse buyer: your job is to make it as easy as possible, as you would for a sixth-grader.

I have said that our readers are human beings. This means that they would rather feel then think. The emotions they like to feel most are hate, distrust, sexual desire and vicarious violence. They also like to feel patriotic and victorious, but these emotions are secondary.

The sex and the violence we handle adequately in our news items and photographs. It is your job to supply, regularly, objects for their hatred and distrust.

We have found through long and successful experience that the most effective method of arousing their hate is to make them feel they have been gypped, or fooled, or betrayed. Here are specific instances, which can be used repeatedly at certain intervals, with only minor changes of approach:

1. *Our so-called Allies* (so-called is a useful phrase). They are unreliable and ungrateful. We spend x million dollars on this and that and that (figures are always available) and what do they do for it? For us? Our readers never fail to respond to the Sucker Sam and Money Down the Drain approach. What they will not tolerate is any evidence to the contrary. It might dilute their anger.

2. *Liberals,* i.e., intellectuals, do-gooders, bleeding-hearts, fuzzy thinkers, etc. You might think that this was

flogging a dead horse—certainly it had the best mileage in the early fifties when Joe McCarthy wrote most of the copy. The public had a taste for blood, and liberal blood tastes best. But even now, where there is admittedly a tendency in certain quarters of government and business to recognize and utilize the "egghead," the arty-pinko-liberal bunch are always good for a laugh. One of the most useful angles now, I think, is that they're always the ones to scream for talks with Russia, more foreign aid, more schoolhouses, etc., at the expense of our security. But lay off the scientists.

3. *The United Nations.* You can't miss on this one for getting folks mad. Foreigners living off us and forced on us. Doubtful loyalties. Haven for spies. Nothing but talk, talk, talk—best possible forum for Soviet propaganda. Pick up little things, like special UN privileges which honest Americans don't have: tax-free, parking, immunity, etc. Play up any incident involving a delegate or employee, stressing alien ways, nuisance-value, taxpayers' burden, etc. Also, their luxurious standard of living contrasted, say, with a New York cab-driver, or such.

4. *Diplomats.* Although the faith of our readers in our foreign service should not be wholly undermined at this point, the average American likes to take pot shots at diplomats in general (as above). Fancy-pants, lad-di-da kind of thing, superior types who talk but don't act, live high, etc., etc. Here again we touch the core of Daily Ruse philosophy: Action, of whatever nature, is superior to thought. Never mind the folderols and the arguments, the buts and ifs: leave them to the longhairs of the leftist press and diplomatic conferences. It's American to act: Hit hard and let the chips fall. Call a spade a spade. Give it to 'em straight. Diplomacy—fancy talk—is negotiation,

and negotiation is concession. Americans can neither con-
ceed nor compromise. This is where national pride comes
in. The U.S. stands for moral values, other nations for self-
interest.

5. *States Rights.* Holler about them, whenever possible.
Most New Yorkers come from other states in the union,
and nothing makes them madder than the idea the federal
government's mixing in their affairs.

6. *Socialism.* See above, re angle of government control
of the people. Push this one for all it's worth, all the time.
We're for social benefits, sure, but any evidence of government planning in health, education or welfare is creeping
socialism. There are a lot of subdivisions under this, like
progressive education, group medicine, federal support of
educational TV, fluoridation, etc., etc.

It will, of course, be obvious to you, that any deals or
cozying up with socialist countries should evoke editorial
alarm and outrage. Remember always to equate socialism
with communism. You and I may know they're not the
same things, but the point is to make our readers believe
they are. If a labor government comes in England you may
have to soft-pedal for a while, but jump on anything that
looks like it's going to hamper private interests. The pitch
is that England may be an ally, but go easy on sharing
secrets with socialists: they might end up in the Kremlin.

We have, over the years, successfully built up a distrust
of the British, rooted in old grudges of the Irish, snubbed
Americans, etc., etc., so it doesn't take much to fan it.
There is a strong attachment to the British royal family,
and we don't kick that around, but Americans always feel
better when the English look inferior—they've been galled
since 1776 by the English assumption of superiority. Besides, they don't like the accent. It sounds educated.

7. *Corruption.* Anger and resentment are easily roused by suggestions of malfeasance in government, whether it is federal, state, or municipal. These are pleasurable emotions for most people because by focusing guilt on others, they remain superior in virtue. Everybody likes to see somebody else get caught for the vices practiced by themselves. In any case it is our duty as a patriotic newspaper primarily concerned with the welfare of our citizens to bring such instances of corruption to light. In spite of the fact that many of our readers are Democrats, there is a certain advantage in exposing Democrats rather than Republican corruption because then you catch the liberals, do-gooders, intellectuals, etc., on the same hook. Democratic corruption has a sinister core of purpose; Republican corruption is usually just plain stupidity.

Because the Ruse is so easy to read and appeals to the simplest human instincts, a large proportion of its readers are in the following categories: the Irish, second-generation minorities like the Italian, German, Czech, etc.; the American Legion and other patriotic groups; labor and white-collar workers; high school (as against college) graduates. Because of its innate conservatism and unswerving battle against Communism, the Ruse appeals strongly to Catholics also. It is therefore obvious that our uncompromising, hard-hitting honesty must not be expended on these groups. On the contrary, all unflattering references to any or all of these groups or persons must be omitted.

On no account and at no time, criticize the Irish, the Catholics, the Jews, the police force or bus-drivers. It is permissible on occasion to take issue with Protestants: they include a number of liberals and anyway, they're not well organized. It is in any event better policy to pick on individuals instead of groups, with one notable exception: the Americans for Democratic Action. We have managed to establish them as a leftist and subversive group over the years and people would be disappointed to find them harmless.

Well, Ed, that's all for now. Happy hunting, sharp writing, and kick 'em in the teeth!

Yours,
Al

4

UNAMERICAN AFFAIRS

In this clearer and freer air, the poisoned climate of McCarthy recedes into distance, blurring our shame in mist. But it was not so long ago that Americans were afraid to say what they believed or write what they thought, and when the best record a man could have was one free of commitment to any idea or ideal. It was a time when men were called Communists if they had loyalist sympathies in the Spanish civil war, contributed to Russian relief in World War II, subscribed to the *Nation,* or had once met a Communist. It was a time when men in high office could speak of Democrats and traitors in one breath, and when a man who had voted for Roosevelt was suspect for that reason only. It was a time when the brave were penalized and the cowardly rewarded, when the primitives in our society were exalted, and the civilized scorned. It was a low time, a mean time, and a dangerous time for Americans; and the good men who did not speak up were as guilty as the bad men who did.

After three years of the bland diet of convalescence, the body of reason has largely recovered. But this does not mean that the virus is still not there. It merely means that the civilized are speaking again and the primitives without a voice or a focus. The country now needs the minds that were reviled and the voices that were stilled, for they were—and are—its strength.

But to immunize us against a recurrence of the disease that flourished on fear and ignorance and cowardice, a booster shot from time to time—the innoculation of memory—might serve some purpose.

Here are three echoes of those years: One is the portrait of a man who, by passive non-commitment, spread the contagion: another concerns three Americans who drew strength from it; and the third is the diagnosis of a foreigner in our midst.

Public Servant

If things hadn't broken the way they did in November, 1952, Cyrus H. Featherbridge might still be a GS 11 at $5,940 a year in one of the sections of the Department of State instead of the Acting Chief of his section at $8,360. This sudden rise to power surprised him almost as much as it surprised everybody else, for several reasons.

Chief among them was the dismissal or resignation of three of his superiors who had been found guilty of offenses ranging from the abandonment of China to expressions of distaste for the word "team." One had even been judged a security risk, although neither he nor any of his colleagues knew why. In any case, Cyrus moved up if for no other reason than that his file had absolutely nothing in it. Nothing, that is, except the facts of his education, his progression up the Civil Service scale and his marriage. Cyrus had never signed a report, written an opinion, evolved a plan, or instigated an action. It was a perfect file.

Consistent with this perfection was the fact that few people ever remembered meeting Cyrus. Although he had the normal complement of features and wore glasses, he was faceless. His clothes were equally indeterminate. The only thing you might remember was his voice: dry, precise, issuing from behind the thin bridge of his nose. He cleared his throat quite often and had a habit (maddening to his secretary) of tapping the desk with his pencil. In the cafeteria another foible was apparent: He pushed the various ingredients of his dish around the plate, patting them into molds before eating them.

Cyrus was a hard and conscientious worker, and his former superiors had counted on him for meticulous attention to detail; but they were frequently exasperated by his refusal to commit himself on any question, however minor. His stock answers to the question "What do you think about this?" were: "I think it needs more study," or, "We're not quite sure of the sources, are we?" or "NEA and FE better have a look at it." They rarely invited him to their houses because he appeared to have no interests beyond the office and no sense of humor.

Yet now that everything was changed, it was men like Cyrus who were referred to by those who attacked the treasonable and disloyal as "one of the many faithful, loyal government servants," and "the backbone of our service."

It was fortunate for the Featherbridges that they had never lived in Georgetown, now discredited as the effete and messy refuge of the Acheson gang, foreign diplomats and homosexuals. Instead, they owned a small brick house in the leafy suburb of Bethesda, where their children could play with nice neighbors instead of with the dirty colored children of Georgetown and where Cyrus, in a room off the garage, could indulge his hobby of carving ship models. Everything about the house spoke of the good, solid American Way.

The Featherbridges had, it is true, once owned a color reproduction of one of Picasso's blue period (a boy and a horse) paintings, but had given it away to a niece who was getting married. Quite aside from Picasso's bad name, they had never really liked the painting; it was a wedding present from a painter-cousin who, they were thankful, lived abroad. She had made them rather nervous during all the investigations because she had voted three times for Norman Thomas, and Ethel Featherbridge was sure that if it had ever come out it would have done Cyrus no good.

In his new position of responsibility Cyrus was changing subtly. He had become fussier and more dictatorial (always on small points of office procedure), cleared his throat oftener, and kept more documents on his desk, for the simple reason that he had no one to pass them on to. This was a worry to him, for it meant that ultimately some action had to be taken where formerly he could just initial and pass on. Cyrus solved this problem by holding regular meetings (at eight-thirty Wednesday mornings, to the anguish of his staff) in which he could sample the opinions of his subordinates and then adopt the majority view. He made a point of keeping a stenographic record of all the comments made, in case at some future time he should be held personally responsible for some decision.

It might be said that Ethel Featherbridge was on the whole happier about his advancement than he was, for she did not suffer the one nagging pang of conscience that Cyrus did. His failure to testify to the good character of his closest colleague, Harbison, had tipped the scales—in those days of accusations, trials, and dismissals—in a case notable for its ambiguity and arbitrariness. What Cyrus had actually done was to answer the question of the

investigators as to whether he knew of any disloyal opinions held, or remarks made, by Harbison, by saying that
his colleague had once praised the public housing program. It was the only time he had ever committed himself
in his life, and it would forever disturb his peace.

The brotherhood of hate: three portraits

The days of Cyrus Featherbridge are gone. He may still exist in the minor corridors of government, but he reaps no rewards now for his total caution even though it may serve as a guarantee against small trouble.

But the primitives still exist here, as they do in every society; sometimes dominating their society, as they did under Hitler, sometimes supporting it, as they do a Strijdom or Nasser, and sometimes disrupting it, as they did with Joseph McCarthy. Primitives are equipped by ignorance and fed on hate, and when they have no one to bind them into a whole, to lead and to succor them, they belong to fringe societies without real power or nurse their directionless anger alone.

This is what our primitives, now largely impotent, do at this time. And this is what they will continue to do so long as our government is strong enough to lead us towards sanity and peace.

But though they may belong now to a period piece, they should not be wholly forgotten. For they are Americans, and some of them might even be your neighbors.

So here are three of them, without a symbol or savior.

1

Agnes MacMillan Worthington is formidable. It is doubtful whether her Revolutionary ancestor, Major General MacMillan, struck more terror on the battlefield than she does at a convention. It is also doubtful whether such feminine adjuncts as ribbons, orchids, and flowered hats could be put to more frightening use than on Agnes Worthington's person. They are then as beguiling as cannon.

Agnes Worthington could not always have been like that. Indeed, there are photographs of her as a young woman which show her as comely and mild, if rather stately in proportions. It is hard to see how two curved and girlish lips could contract to the rat trap that now serves as her mouth, how that gentle bosom could become a barricade, and how those doelike eyes could have shrunk to pinpoints glinting behind pixie glasses. But they have.

It is possibly the clearest of all examples of the influence of mind over matter. Agnes Worthington's mind has been closing ever since puberty. It opened a little then, but what it saw was so distasteful that it shut up again. It is now just big enough to encompass three concepts: the superiority of Agnes Worthington over other women; the superiority of the MacMillian family over all other families, races, and nations; and the superiority of woman over man.

The first superiority is easily arrived at. Agnes Worthington has never made a mistake. She looked at no man before she married the coming young banker who came, and looked at no other man after. She never touches liquor, and she is the president of her local chapter.

The second superiority is also easily arrived at. The MacMillan family came over on the Mayflower. It distinguished itself in the two major battles for the formation of America. It never married foreigners. And it produced Agnes.

No explanation of the third concept is needed. Both the men in her family—her husband, Hiram, and her son, Ralph—are putty in her hands. Hiram is now an alcoholic (nonviolent); Ralph, at twenty-six, is studying tribal customs of various remote peoples as a respectable excuse for the collection of pornographia. The first command that Hiram ever gave to Agnes was his last. He told her to undress. As for Ralph, he worships his mother. "My best girl," he calls her.

These three concepts have, of course, their inevitable corollaries. Agnes Worthington considers most women weak in that they respond to stimuli which she abhors. She finds all men fundamentally base and stupid in that they respond to women.

It is no wonder, therefore, that she has risen so high in the ancestral organization to which she belongs by birth, or that she fights so ferociously and unceasingly against all those ideas and forces which do not correspond to her own.

These alien ideas and forces arouse in Agnes physiological symptoms which in other women would be attributed to sex. One has only to mention such words as Negro, Jew, planning, Social Security, Europe, Democrats, liberals, United Nations, or civil rights for Agnes Worthington's breathing to quicken, her face to flush, her eyes to flash, and her flesh to tremble. Oddly enough the word "revolution" has the same effect.

It is perhaps a paradox that the prevailing emotion of this redoubtable woman is fear. This female fortress is in a state of chronic terror of siege. Considering her premise of superiority, this is hard to explain. Possibly she feels that the forces of right and light are diminishing to such an extent that only the greatest vigilance can preserve her kind.

That may be why conventions are so good for her disposition (not to speak of Hiram's). Here, in some great hall in some great city, Agnes Worthington sees herself multiplied a thousandfold. Here are the cohorts of sanity, all together: a solid phalanx of orchid-covered bosoms and nodding hats. Here is the voice of reason, issuing from rightful lips. Here is the stronghold of the strong, the women without men, the blood of the pure. An almost religious feeling overwhelms Agnes Worthington at these moments.

There are, of course, some flaws: women who now and then rise up to protest the majority rulings; women, no doubt, who have come into contact with the virus of internationalism, the poison of socialism, or the opiate of sex. To Agnes, they are traitors to their kind. It is always with intense gratification that she witnesses their defeats. And the period of their greatest defeats was, of course, when that wonderful Senator McCarthy became the living symbol of all that was American and right and good. Never had Agnes been more suffused with the pure wrath of the righteous than when his words rang out to save the nation. And if anyone had told this daughter of revolution who despised revolution that she was pursuing a course that could lead to revolution and wreck the nation, she would have considered him insane.

But then, she never saw that kind of person anyway; although he would have been her great-great-grandfather's friend.

II

If you should come across Charlie Mattson and his family barbecuing in the back yard of their Darien home, you would think they came straight off the cover of the *Saturday Evening Post*. There is the jolly father-chef in his apron, the pretty—but not too pretty—wife in slacks, the twelve-year old boy with the T shirt and the crew cut, and the teen-age girl in heavy white socks and loafers, blue-jeaned, sweatered and pony-tailed. They appear to be having a genuinely good time.

There is no reason, really, why they shouldn't. Charlie has a good job in a factory sub-contracted to a defense plant, his family is healthy, and he is a pillar of his American Legion Post, the Presbyterian church, the Kiwanis and the weekly poker group. One reason for this is his good nature, another is his repertory of jokes, mainly for male consumption. Charlie rolls 'em in the aisles.

Yet Charlie is one of those men who was, whether he admits it or not, happiest in the war. He got overseas late in the game, but not too late to taste the liberation of Paris and the advance into Germany, and he can never forget the excitement and fulfilment of either. Nor can he forget the German girl he shacked up with after the surrender, in the months of occupation that followed. Ruins, starvation and all, he found the Germans very much to his liking, and he joined a number of other Americans in wondering why the hell they had fought the Krauts instead of the Frogs. Fundamentally, the Germans had the right ideas, and one of them was plumbing.

The nearest he could come to those war days now were bull sessions at the Post, where the men would reminisce about the war and the women they had. But the years after the war were a letdown to men like Charlie. They were conscious of a great lack: there was no place to go, nothing to do, no direction, really. They were disgusted with the untidiness and frustration of civilian life, and they began to blame it on all sorts of things, beginning with socialism (that bastard Truman and his goddam Fair Deal) and ending with Jews, foreigners, do-gooders, pinkos and longhairs.

It was small wonder then that when the Junior Senator from Wisconsin began raising his voice in 1952, Charlie began to listen. Here, at last, was a call to action, a new kind of war for good Americans to wage. McCarthy gave men like Charlie a motive and a function: to rid this country of the traitors in its midst, to hunt down the enemy, to restore America to its rightful owners and guardians. The bugle had sounded and Charlie Mattson joined the colors.

But things have died down a bit since, partly because most of the reds had been smoked out, and partly because there was nobody left in the government who had the guts to keep up the fight against subversion. For there was no doubt in Charlie's mind that his country was in constant danger of penetration, that the wrong people were getting back into power, and that the only reason the Russians were ahead of us was that they stole our secrets.

But what can you do when people are dumb? Make money and mind your own business and tell your children what the score is. If folks can't realize, for instance, that this whole integration business is one more communist plot and that the Supreme Court is playing right into their hands, it's their funeral.

III

Emily is a widow of fifty who lives with her seventy-year-old mother in a small town not far from Shreveport, Louisiana. If one were to describe Emily, a recurrent word would be "confused." Wispy and disorganized in dress and manner, she has the look of a woman who has never known what hit her. Since her husband died ten years ago of undiagnosed diabetes, she has kept house for her deaf and irritable mother in a mansion too large for them on an income too small for it. When she looks at the indifferent young colored girl who cleans once a week for outrageous wages, Emily remembers bitterly the smiling servants of her youth.

Now she does most of the work, cooking flavorless snacks for the two of them and waiting for the hot days to pass. Aside from the church, of which she is an active member, Emily's only real diversion is the radio, and she listens regularly every day to at least five soap operas. Her only other fixed radio date is during suppertime, when she listens to the news presented and commented on by a man who seems to make clear to her all sorts of things she never understood before.

Until five years ago, when she first tuned him in by accident, Emily had avoided listening to the news because it upset and confused her. There were so many things going on in the world, usually dreadful, and you never could make head or tail of them. But this man could. He took her into his confidence with his kind, quiet voice, and told her why things were as they were. The reason they were living so poorly was the taxes, and the money for the taxes was all Wasted by the Government and Given Away to Foreigners, and food too, so that people like Emily and her mother had to eat out of cans. And Minturn had died of diabetes because the Democrats were trying to bring in socialized medicine. And the Negroes were so rich and uppity because the government was trying to make everybody equal, as if anybody was. And there were traitors just everywhere trying to take America away from the Americans, right under their noses, just like Senator McCarthy said. All these things were clear now, and the dim inchoate anger that had smoldered so long in Emily's breast was burning bright and sharp. She wished there was something she could do to help.

Agnes, Charlie, and Emily, left to themselves, are three individuals worlds apart in character, background, capacity; faceless and lost in the great host of their countrymen.

Each by himself is without direction or destination, his motion through life not unlike the movement of a mote in the sunlight or of a bacillus in fluid.

They share, however, two profound emotions: hate and fear. Since they cannot create, their outlet is destruction. And they will listen to anyone who can define the thing to be destroyed. And in the case of these three—or three times three times three and so on in a long, unhappy process of multiplication—it can be the voice of one man speaking to their viscera and impelling them along one course. So mobs are born.

The friendliest people in the world,
fundamentally

The men were in the library after dinner when the host, a public-relations man, collared the visiting Danish scholar.

"What beats me," he said, "is why all you people over there are scared of us. It's easy enough to see why the Russians should scare you. They're a primitive, aggressive race sitting right on your neck. But look at us. Did we ever want a war? It's all we can do to keep an army going. Why, we're the friendliest people in the world, fundamentally."

"That is what we always believed," said the pink-cheeked young man. The American looked at him sharply.

"Why the past tense? We're no different than we ever were."

"I am sorry, sir, but we believe that you are. You see—" and here he blushed—"we believe you are a violent race."

"Violent? Whoever put that idea in your head?"

"It is what we see—what we read. Those comic books for children—"

The American laughed, slapping his guest on the back. "Oh, those. My dear young man, my two boys were addicts

and look at them now. Good clean young Americans, normal as they come. There's a lot of hysteria about that."

"I have heard, sir, that over twenty million crime comic
books are published every month, and that every day on
television there are many shootings and beatings. And
over the radio, when I listened to an investigation by
Senators, I heard from people and doctors what they were
doing to delinquency."

"There's no proof, absolutely no proof. Sure, neurotic
kids get ideas, maybe, but there's no proof."

"There was in these hearings," the young Scandinavian
persisted earnestly, "a publisher of crime comics. A Senator held up to him the cover of one of his books showing
a man holding in one hand an ax and in the other the cut-
off head of a blond woman. And the Senator asked, 'Is
this in good taste?' and the publisher said, yes, it was, for
a cover of a horror comic book, but that it would be bad
taste if the man were holding the head higher so that the
neck would show with the blood dripping from it. And
the Senator said, 'You have blood dripping from the
mouth. You believe that is not violent?' "

"Sure, it's terrible," said the American, "but they've got
a code now."

"If fifty million children see things like this every day,
do you not think they will feel less about shooting and
murder and rape? They will be so used to violence that it
does not seem like violence any more." As the American
was occupied in lighting his cigarette, the Danish scholar
went on, "Your juvenile crime has risen greatly in the last
year, I read."

"Plenty of factors. Slums. Broken families . . . My dear
fellow, don't blame it all on TV and comics. Anyway, you
can't stop them."

"We have," said the Dane. "We think they are like the narcotics trade, only for the mind. We forbid them."

"Couldn't do that here, my boy. Freedom of the press."

An American journalist came to join them, hearing "press." The host said, "Al, this young man thinks we're a violent race. Basing it all on TV and comic books. I told him—"

The Dane interrupted, "No sir, I did not mean only—"

"I agree," cut in the journalist, and then to the Dane, "What else makes you think that?"

"Oh, many things. Please, I like the American people very much, you are generous and kind, but this I speak of is something that is new, that was not before. I am think- ing of your high-school students in their black leather jackets. They are loud and angry and dirty-mouthed and have no politeness at all. They do not seem to believe in anything. They are violent, like young storm troopers. And your sound, it is always too loud. It is violent to the ear. And your bus-drivers and motorists—they are always angry and brutal. I do not see any self-control anywhere —in the children or in the old. I have not anywhere seen discipline."

"Oh, cities are always like that," said the public-relations man. "You ought to get out into the country more. That's where you'll find more people decent and friendly."

The journalist grinned. "Did you see a TV show about a month ago called "Thunder on Sycamore Street?"

"Yeah, Ruth and I did. Thought it was good, but over- written and hysterical."

To the Dane the journalist said: "It was about a nice little suburban community, where all the neighbors in one street ganged together to throw out another neighbor be- cause he was an ex-convict. They threw stones at him."

The young student shook his head. "That is too much. Surely it is not possible here."

"I didn't think so either . . . until I heard a radio documentary on Mrs. Peress and her Queens PTA."

"Mrs. Peress? The wife of the army dentist who was charged with having been a Communist?"

"Yes. Well, Edward Morgan—that was the commentator—was interviewing the mothers and neighbors and PTA members concerned, and what came out made 'Sycamore Street' seem like a kids' party. Apparently at that meeting in Queens grown women screamed at Mrs. Peress: 'The Oath! The Oath! Make her take the Oath!' Mrs. Peress told Morgan she'd never seen such 'undemocracy'; she didn't think it was possible here. She said it was like people screaming 'Confess! Confess!' at the Salem witches. From all accounts, these ordinary housewives and mothers behaved like a crazed mob. The whole neighborhood was rotten with fear."

"Well now, Al, people *are* worried about Communist infiltration, you know. You can't exactly blame them."

"But what are they afraid of, for heaven's sake?" exploded the journalist. "That their children might be subverted by contact with the children of a woman who was married to a man who might have been a Communist? Mrs. Peress wasn't teaching. She'd apparently done a perfectly loyal job editing the PTA magazine."

"If you'll excuse me," said the young Dane, "I think there is one cause for all this violence."

"One?" asked the journalist wryly.

"What I have been thinking is that your people are so soft physically—their life is so soft—that they must be violent in other ways. They do not walk or work in the open air or exercise as our young people do. They eat too much and they ride everywhere and they sit in hot rooms looking at things. So they must put their energy into their feeling. It has no physical way out."

"You may have something there," said the public-relations man. "My God, you ought to hear the squawks from my boys when they can't have the car for a party half a mile away!"

The journalist turned to the Danish scholar. "What do you think of the Army-McCarthy hearing?"

Here the young foreigner blushed deeply. "I think I should not speak about this," he said. "I think that is the direct product of this violence you speak of. It is a violence against truth, against morality. It is this violence that creates and supports a McCarthy. Isn't it really this kind of violence that scares you people more than any other?"

"Look here, Al," said the publicist, "don't try to tell us that everybody in the world is honest and moral except us!"

"Certainly not. But we're the only ones who think we are."

"Is it possible, perhaps," said the young Dane hesitantly, "that you cannot have power without violence?"

"It is possible that you can," said the journalist, "and we made a good start in that direction. But now . . . Well, it depends on how many of us wear black leather jackets, break the windows of neighbors, scream 'Take the Oath!' and violate the truth. Isn't that what you're scared of, really, you people in Europe? That and the H-bomb?"

"I wouldn't worry too much," said the public-relations man, patting the scholar paternally on the back. "Just re-

member our boys in Korea—they were wonderful to the
kids there. Fundamentally, we're the kindest people in
the world."

Someone else had engaged the young Dane's attention,
and the American took his compatriot to one side, saying
in a low voice, "Too bad—sounds like he had a dose of
red propaganda along the line."

"Think so?" said the journalist as he drifted away.

III

THE ARTS: SELLING
THE PUBLIC

THE SMALL SCREEN

The magic box

Time: A.D. 2000
Place: A heath, blasted
Characters: A VERY OLD MAN
              A STUDENT
The *student* is making notes on what looks like papyrus
with what looks like a stylus.

STUDENT: You say, old man, that Americans looked at the
magic box from two to three hours every day. But why
would a people need to be entertained every day? What
did they lack?

OLD MAN: I do not know what they lacked, but I suspect it was will—or direction. They were sitting still, rather than moving forward. And anyway, it was not a question of what people needed. They did not ask for television; it was given them.

STUDENT: But surely the desire was there. You say that people get the kind of government they want. Do they not also get the kind of leisure and recreation they want?

OLD MAN: Not entirely. You see, there was a deception in the whole matter of the magic box. People thought that television was free because they did not have to pay for what they saw. But they paid heavily, without knowing it.

STUDENT: I don't think I wholly understand. In what ways, old man?

OLD MAN: Well you see, what they saw was almost entirely determined by what they would buy, in the way of goods. Hour after hour, day after day, year after year, they were urged to buy what they very often did not need, because that was the basis of the American economy; which—as you know—was very successful as long as it lasted. It was only in the latter years of that era that the masters of television acknowledged a deeper purpose: the need to educate and inform, without selling.

STUDENT: But how else did people pay for television, beyond having to buy what they did not need?

OLD MAN: They paid in boredom; they paid in satiety; they paid in passivity; they paid in the dulling of perception between true and false. They paid above all in the strength and imagination of their children. They destroyed fantasy by feeding them artifice. And they made them callous to violence by exposing them daily to violence. Of the sins committed by the masters of television—and, of necessity, by the producers of goods —this was the greatest: that for decades they either ignored the true needs of children or substituted false desires based on adult indulgences.

STUDENT: You mean there was really nothing for children on the magic box?

OLD MAN: Oh yes. Out of a hundred hours, thirty minutes of tender fun or illumination; extinguished in time by an avalanche of trash. Some people tried to give children what they needed, but most of the time they failed. It was more profitable to sell to adults.

STUDENT: But why, for the sake of the nation's children, did not the government take control?

OLD MAN: (*laughing harshly*) The government! Dear lad, to suggest that in those days was tantamount to treason. It was one of the paradoxes of the American way of life that while they prided themselves on having a government by the people, of the people, and for the people, government itself was considered against the people. Business, which was people, could and did interfere with, affect, and often control the lives of most Americans. But government, which was no less people, could not attempt any regulation, however necessary to the national survival, without outraged protest.

STUDENT: What a strange society!

OLD MAN: (*shaking his head sadly*) Yes, indeed. But in many ways a wonderful society. If only they had trusted themselves to be strong! (*he lapses into revery*)

STUDENT: Excuse me for bothering you, old man, but for purposes of this history I would like very much to be specific about what Americans actually saw every day on the magic box. Do you remember well enough to give me a sort of category?

OLD MAN: Only too well, my boy, only too well. They are branded on this old brain. Let's see, let's see—where shall we start?

STUDENT: Could we not start with the hours of the day, or the days of the week, or some such measurement of time?

OLD MAN: If we started with the hours of the day, we should be sitting here for weeks, and I am too old for that. I will try instead to give you a general idea of what was impressed on the eyes and ears and minds of eighty millions of Americans in that time. What they saw most, I believe, was a kind of play called a "Western." They concerned good men and bad men who rode horses over magnificent country and decided issues by shooting each other. They were all very much alike in that they bore no resemblance to what used to be the pioneer West of the United States except in the matter of clothes and horses. They provided, I remember, the ideal escape from real problems, and total relief from thought. They were able to sell a great amount of goods because they appealed to everyone from the President of the United States to a child of six. As a matter of fact, I enjoyed the horses at times myself.

STUDENT: (*writing*) Westerns. . . .

OLD MAN: Ah yes, and put down that these Westerns had a profound and prolonged effect on the children of the United States, who, from the age of two, went around with belts and holsters containing two guns, which they brandished freely.

STUDENT: (*writing*) Warlike race. . . .

OLD MAN: I believe the things Americans saw most after

Westerns were what they called variety shows—a sort of mixed entertainment centering around one personality, or a singer. I seem to remember especially some man who sold cars and lived on the talents of others; and another man—a singer—who never got excited about anything. They were extremely popular.

STUDENT: Can you tell me why?

OLD MAN: I never knew why myself. I suppose it is because Americans then wished to be soothed beyond anything else in the world. "Tranquilized" was the word. If they did not take pills, they listened to this singer. The results of both, of course, were debilitating.

STUDENT: But if that was so, old man, then why did the Americans want to see so much shooting and killing on their television? Surely this is not soothing.

OLD MAN: No. It was just the other side of the picture. Every man has violence within him. But if his sole aim in life is to be amiable and friendly, passive and popular, then this deep need must find other outlets. If a man is not active or creative, he must dream of action and destruction. They called it relaxation in those days, or "release from tension." But again, it was release from thought, and therefore soothing.

STUDENT: What else did they like, old man?

OLD MAN: Well, they liked anything to do with money. Great sums of money. They were given away on television to people who could remember a great many unrelated facts at the right moments. Fortunes in goods and cash were bestowed on people who could place a song, guess a price, or be victims of catastrophe. An earlier American myth was that any man who worked hard could become a millionaire or President. But in the age of television, any man with the right answer could win a fortune. This was the new myth: that wealth required no effort.

STUDENT: (*wistfully*) What a golden age!

OLD MAN: There was, too, I remember, an extraordinary form of drama called the soap opera. . . .

STUDENT: Soap opera?

OLD MAN: Yes. Because the makers of soap paid for them, not because they had music. Many million women watched them every day, and wept.

STUDENT: Wept? Why?

OLD MAN: Because their troubles were slight compared to those of the characters, who lived from calamity to calamity; and they wept from relief.

STUDENT: But what were these dramas about?

OLD MAN: They were about very stupid people who were either good or bad. But there were good and bad in very special ways. . . .

STUDENT: What ways, old man?

OLD MAN: Well, all good women did housework all day and drank coffee. All bad women had careers, flirted with men and drank cocktails.

STUDENT: And the men?

OLD MAN: I seem to remember that the bad men were usually cultivated, witty, and upper-class; and all the good men were dull, faithful and humorless. You see, in America there was nothing funny about love, or sex. It was either nobly matrimonial, ignobly adulterous, or painfully adolescent. But it was never amusing.

STUDENT: Poor Americans!

OLD MAN: What is more, the inhabitants of soap operas never read books, although judges sometimes referred to volumes of law. And I do not remember a single interior with books except the home of a retired professor,

who was a social and intellectual snob and highly dis-
agreeable. He liked first editions and hated plain folk.

STUDENT: Then learning was never popular?

OLD MAN: Not until too late, my son.

STUDENT: What about the young in these strange plays?

OLD MAN: The young—they called them "teen-agers"—
had no interests but what they called "dating." The
younger boys and girls had no interest but sports. I seem
to remember only one little boy who did not play
games, and he had a bad heart.

STUDENT: But were these people then reflections of living
Americans?

OLD MAN: In a sense, yes. Particularly in their manner of
behavior, for neither the young nor the old nor the good
nor the bad had any control over their emotions. I remember them as chronic hysterics: storming, weeping,
threatening, terrified in situations requiring only a grain
of common sense.

STUDENT: And you say Americans were really like that?

OLD MAN: No, I would not say that much. But I do say
that the sign of an intelligent people is their ability to
control emotions by the application of reason, and there
was a time near the end when the Americans preferred
their primitives.

STUDENT: But were there no other dramas than these and
"Westerns," old man?

OLD MAN: Ah yes, indeed, my son. There were ten thousand plays which forced life—or an approximation of
life—into an hour or thirty minutes, neatly concluded;
there were ten thousand comedies in which people who
could not exist found themselves in situations which
could not exist—

STUDENT: (*interrupting*) Were they funny?

OLD MAN: They were accompanied by the mechanical laughter of absent people, so it was hard to say. I believe I remember laughing once or twice, but you see, my boy, humor died in that last era. All that was left was tricks and jokes—I believe the word then was "gags."

STUDENT: But old man, all these things you mention were frivolous. Was there nothing serious or elevating on the magic box?

OLD MAN: Oh yes, my boy, indeed; but a trickle compared to this avalanche. Once in a while there was a strong, true play, finely conceived and presented. And some brave men spoke the news truly, and others discussed life truly. And there were many excellent studies of the living world and the peoples inhabiting it. But nearly all these things were crowded in one day—the day when goods were not sold, the day when men were supposed to examine their conscience and enrich their souls. But when six days are devoted to stilling conscience and starving the mind, the seventh alone cannot redress the balance. It was equivalent to worshiping God in public one day a week and forgetting Christian behavior the rest of the time. You see, the masters of television made this limited outward show of performing a function which should have been a daily obligation to the people. . . .

STUDENT: And what do you call this obligation?

OLD MAN: I call it to enlighten, to inform, to stimulate, to educate.

STUDENT: Never to entertain?

OLD MAN: No man needs more than an hour of entertainment a day, if that. But all men, and certainly all Americans in that day, needed education—constant and unremitting—for the leadership which the world so desperately needed.

STUDENT: And they did not get it.

OLD MAN: No, they did not get it. Because they believed more in the selling of goods than in the saving of souls. The magic box was the greatest key to wisdom man ever devised. But they made it a toy, for profit. It was, you see, the age of wasted miracles.

The child before the set

I am sorry for the children who are brought up on television; not so much for the fare they receive, which is
often of abysmal quality, as for the hours they lose. For
while it is grotesque enough that healthy adults be "entertained" for three hours a day for six days a week (the
seventh being mercifully reserved for enlightenment) it
is an act of destruction that children should kill time,
which is the most precious thing they possess: time to
dream, time to imagine, time to make. Until a child can
meet reality, he must live in fantasy. But he must create
his own fantasy. And it is television's primary damage
that it provides ten million children with the same fantasy, ready-made and on a platter. Nor is this, with very
rare exceptions, the fruitful fantasy of poets or artists but
the unreal world of television itself, which bears no relation to that of a child but which envelops him, willy-
nilly, in a false adult vision which, in turn, is not even
truly adult. And on this infinitely sensitive and apparently
unerasable recording-tape of the child's mind is printed a
shadow world of blurred values, where the only reality
is the product Mom must buy.
   This need not be so. Television could be the great

teacher and the great revealer to children, and I hope I live till the day when it fulfills its miraculous function as a third eye. But now I can think only of the killing of hours, and remember the hours of one child who grew before television pre-empted them.

In my childhood the days were not regimented. After school and before a homework evening, the time was our own, for us to fill as we chose. In school we were groups, at home we were single; and it never occurred to my parents to arrange my social day with organized activity. They felt that a good school, an affectionate home, and a consistent standard of ethics were enough. The rest was up to us, my brother and me.

I cannot presume that our life was typical, because my parents were making music all day, teaching or playing together or rehearsing for concerts, my mother at the piano, my father with the violin. In time my brother used the piano when it was free, and there were very few hours in my childhood when the air in our home was dead, or empty of meaning. Because of this, the advent of radio, miraculous as we thought it, left us indifferent. What could it give us then that our life could not? What need was there to turn on its scratchy blatancies when musicians like Cortot and Casals and Thibaud came to the apartment and joined my parents in the quintets and trios of Brahms, in Schubert quartets? I remember clearly the exaltation this music brought me, a sense of excitement and glory that often impelled me to tears. And I remember sitting in a corner of the living room watching these musicians play and noticing the transfiguration of their faces, which, a moment before had been—to my childish eyes—neither handsome nor extraordinary. I saw what music did to them and I felt great awe.

This was not, I repeat, a typical home; rather it was a rarely fortunate one. Yet there were still those hours in the afternoon when my parents were teaching or on tour, when my brother, whose five-year seniority then kept us worlds apart, was out or away, and when I fended for myself, often alone. And I know that if television had been in the house I would not have done what I did. I read, voraciously and indiscriminately, nearly a book a day, alternating the *Golden Bough* with *Dotty Dimple,* *Kidnapped* with the *St. Nicholas* magazine. I wrote very bad poems with very deep emotion. I studied Swahili phrases in African adventure stories. I made peculiar figures out of plastecine, I painted messy water-colors of flowers in vases, I practiced the role, patterned on John Barrymore, of Richard III, I tried leaping like Nijinsky in *Spectre de La Rose,* and I spent a considerable amount of time hanging by my knees from a trapeze set in my bedroom door. I liked the feeling.

When I was not engaged in any of these pursuits, I was out on Riverside Drive with a friend, usually standing on a bridge where the freight trains came through beneath in a hissing cloud of white steam, or walking along the Hudson smelling the dampness of rotting piers, or climbing granite mountains blazing with mica. The hours were long and the sun was bright and our heads full of crazy thoughts. Even in our teens, nobody told us to join anything, nobody arranged subscription dances so that we could meet the right boys, and, in fact, we never thought of meeting boys. We were in love with Peter Ibbetson.

What is more—and what I believe to be most relevant of all to the age before television and mass communication in general—I do not remember in all my childhood any commercial preoccupation. We bought what we needed, but nobody sold anything to us. My parents worried, often, about money, for they made little and lived gracefully. But the talk was of meeting bills, not of buying new things. And we were brought up, if not with frugality, then with a stern sense of the value of money and the sin of waste. To want things without needing them was an impulse to be scorned, and the word "material" in describing a person, an epithet.

Listen then to this excerpt from a well-known woman newspaper columnist, Sylvia Porter, writing last year about her eight-year old daughter:

> I began to think carefully about her [she wrote] and the millions of children like her, who are extravagant. It is not an extravagance encouraged by us. Rather, it is an extravagance stimulated by the TV shows they see and radio shows they hear—shows which cajole them into buying things and food on a scale which can be believed only by those living the experience. To Cris and all the boys and girls of her age who are allowed to watch TV during the pre-supper hour, the commercials are often more intriguing than the performances themselves.
>
> They feel they must obey when they are told to "go right out and buy" something. They ask and they nag— and finally, most of us give in.
>
> Again, we are not developing the brand name devotion in the youngsters. It is being pounded into them by the ads they see and hear on every side. They don't eat "a" cereal: they eat such-and-such cereal; they don't drink "a" soft drink; they name it by brand name.
>
> In all seriousness, Cris will tell me that a certain food is "good for me"—and she will tell me why in words that obviously come right out of a commercial. I recall my own childhood; I never asked for a food or drink because it would "help me grow."

[Speaking of her own childhood, Miss Porter wrote:] I think I ate some food in the packages which came with the prizes. Not so with Cris and her friends. They grab the package, extract the price or cut out the gimmick, etc., and that's the end of it. At times, I think that if all the half-consumed boxes of cereal on Americans' pantry shelves right now were collected and shipped overseas, we could solve the hunger problem of a fair-sized nation.

[Then, later] Cris and her friends will actually coo over the color and style of a new car or appliance. In fact I think they're snobbish about it.

After this curdling tale, Miss Porter ends on a happy note. "In short," she concludes, "one decade from today, Cris and her contemporaries will be creating a market in our land, lush and luxurious beyond anything ever seen."

While this may delight the country's economists and the makers of goods, it horrifies me. For it is in effect producing a race which believes that a high standard of living is the final aspiration. I would be more inclined to call it the last ditch.

I am sorry for the children who grow up on television. They don't know what they've missed, or how rich life can be, in the real and imagined world.

The victors and the victims

Whatever television may have done to our children, the mass media have been a bonanza for women; not only as sedation for the harried housewife but for the women working in radio or television itself. We have always been the communicators of the race, but now the small box and the small screen have produced a new kind of female who wields a power, through talk alone, far beyond her individual talents or intelligence.

But where she triumphs, another talker fails. He is the television comedian who can no longer function in a medium that must please all. And if there is any moral in the two following fables, it is that women thrive on exposure and the comic spirit dies from overexposure.

LADY CHATTERER'S LOVERS

In no era could it have been more felicitous for Kitty McCaffery to be born than this one, for it is the first in which women have been paid to talk. This is the most natural and requires the least effort of all feminine activities. And because of the ease of this flow, nobody thought it worth buying until the gods of mass communication realized they had to fill sixteen hours of air seven days a week. It was then that chatter become a commodity.

Kitty started young. Irish and French blood loosened her tongue at the age of three, so that when Father bent over to tickle her under the chin, gurgling "Kitsy Witsy, Daddy's bitsy," she eyed him coldly and said, "I bet you say that to all the girls."

The family was so entranced by her snappy comebacks that whenever friends were in the McCaffery house, Kitty would prance in unbidden, dimples and all, and pipe her little impudences at them. Whether they enjoyed them or not, they gave every evidence of doing so, for Mr. McCaffery was the head of a corporation which—in the tentacular way of such powers—usually touched on some sensitive part of their lives.

By the age of eighteen, Kitty was not only used to audiences but acquainted with most of the celebrities in town, and it was not long before she combined these assets by writing a column for teen-agers in one of the newspapers in which her father happened to hold stock. The fact that she could not write a coherent sentence (transition from item to item was made possible only by the dash or exclamation point), and that her command of verbs was confined to "is" and "said," was irrelevant. She could babble in print every day for five hundred words, a hundred of which were proper names. That was enough.

For a man, the next step would have been political prophecy; but Kitty was attractive, in a Stork Club way, and her career (although not her column) was momentarily interrupted by a husband and child. But Kitty was no fool. Her husband was an account executive with an advertising firm, and it was a happy coincidence that his field was radio and television, especially happy in that electronics could give Kitty what the printed page could not: freedom of garrulity without the painful confinement of syntax.

When Bobby was five, therefore, and Kitty had elevated her column from teen-agers to Broadway (by the insertion of older names and dramatic criticism), she began to conduct a fifteen-minute daily radio program called "Lunch with Kitty." She had a guest every day, and her list ranged from Barbara Ward to a woman who had a secret recipe for popovers. Ostensibly these were interviews. But by the time Kitty got through showing hand-beaded cocktail mats and describing last night's party, Bobby's latest crack, and her friends' latest triumphs, the guest had barely two minutes to speak of isotopes or Kentucky ballads. Deceived by happier experiences with women commentators of more substance and humility, and by Kitty's uncontrollable eagerness to hear of such matters ("Now, tell us all about the wonderful things you're doing for delinquency!"), he or she would finally embark on the topic only to be cut off in the middle of the second sentence. "Oh, isn't this awful," Kitty would say, jingling her many bracelets, "our time's running out."

But *her* time never runs out. Today she has not only "Lunch with Kitty" but two television programs, one a daily "Kitty Corner," unhampered by guests, and one a weekly panel show called "Secret Urge." On the sound assumption that everybody has one, the panel's function is to find out what it is, and Kitty and her colleagues manage inevitably to analyze their own urges as well as the guests'. This is done to the accompaniment of convulsive private merriment, for which they are handsomely paid.

It is really in "Kitty Corner," however, that talk is triumphant. Even for the garrulous, twelve minutes is a long time to fill, but Kitty never feels the need of drawing breath. So much *happens* to her! She knows so many *people!* She sees so many *things!* Drabbo is so *wonderful!*

Gaily, relentlessly, Kitty shares with her large audience every waking moment of her life. These have included the birth of her second child (she looked adorable the morning after in her Daisy Mode bed jacket), the decision to change from double to twin beds, and the state of her husband's pajama tops.

It must be conceded that Kitty can be amusing. It would be virtually impossible not to develop a certain associative quickness, a certain basic adroitness, after thirty years of circulation in an extrovert society, especially for one so shrewd, nerveless, and confident as Kitty.

There, perhaps, is the vital word: confidence. Kitty believes profoundly that what she is and what she does is so fascinating that it must be offered to as wide a public as possible. Since several million people a day listen to her on radio and look at her on television, the public must agree with her.

The captious exceptions are prone to wonder why. If, idly curious, they tune in to her now and then, they see a woman who is neither very pretty nor very intelligent nor very interesting, talking the smallest kind of talk minute after minute. They see a woman without privacy or inhibition engaged in nothing but selling: selling of self. Here is the human department store, its doors wide open, the counters piled with goods, the people streaming in and out. In the window displays are her husband, her children, her family, and what few intimacies her life permits. And the lights are never out, even at night when the store is empty.

It might console the unconverted to believe that Kitty's professional success is achieved at the expense of her personal relationships; that her husband is resentful, her children warped by overexposure, her family wincing in the glare. But such is not the case. They expand like flowers in the sun of her publicity. Her husband has been made vice-president of his firm, her relatives get the best tables at night clubs, and her son is the most popular boy in the class because of his poor scholastic record and limitless supply of TV tickets. Thanks to her and to an age that equates Power with Publicity, they are the new Privileged. When Kitty visits the White House, baptizes a new atomic pile, or covers the latest Congressional inquiry, they are right there, beaming. To no one does it seem strange that they have achieved their eminence solely by existing.

To no one, that is, except the captious few who turn off Kitty's flow when they accidentally tune in on her. But then, she never knows that; and what you don't know, as her uncharitable critics say of Kitty's monumental insensibility, can't hurt you.

NO KIDDING
Memo from a TV Comic to His Former Sponsor

Okay, so you pulled the rug out. I'm not beefing. After twenty-six weeks I can use a rest.

But I am going to beef about what you people are do-

ing to comedy in these United States. You're killing it.
And I don't mean gags, they go on forever. I mean humor.
Real humor. I mean satire—that's humor's Siamese twin,
stuck back to back. And you're killing it because you
haven't any guts. And the reason you haven't any guts is
that you're afraid of losing ten customers in Blackwater
Junction. You have to please everybody so that everybody will buy Buffo. So nobody can make fun of anything that matters because somebody might get sore. The
only thing left for a comic to make fun of is the female
torso and Jack Benny's age. Groucho Marx was dead
right when he said that if Will Rogers were alive today he
wouldn't be on the air. The best cowboy in the world
can't ride herd on the sacred cows. There are just too
damn many of them.

Let me give you an idea of the kind of material I can't
use. (I know because I tried some a few years ago and the
agency threw it out.)

I can't talk in dialect, any dialect—except, maybe
Southern accent. It might offend the Jews, the Irish, the
Negroes, the Anti-Defamation League and umpteen other
organizations. Never mind if people speak like that and
all you want to do is show human beings the way they
are. Dialect is out.

I can't make fun of politics, from the President down.
When the Democrats were in you could get any laughs
you wanted out of FDR and Harry S. and deep freezes
and music critics and especially Eleanor. But try doing
that with this bunch. It's bad taste to get a laugh out of
Republicans. Business is Republican, and you—the sponsor—are business. So no matter how cockeyed things are
at the White House, lay off the great White Father.

In fact, lay off Congress, the Army, the Navy, the Air

Force, and anything which might show our great country with a cinder in its eye or a smudge on its nose. If you don't, you'll get a ton of pressure mail from the American Legion, the D.A.R., the Minute Women, and a pack of other groups around the country composed of people too busy calling themselves patriots to be decent citizens themselves.

If you think I'm exaggerating, ask any censor (excuse me, "continuity acceptance" man) of any network about the letters he gets every day. You would think the whole country was one lunatic fringe—thousands and thousands of dopes and psycopaths and busybodies who don't want anybody else to see what they don't like. Sure, a lot of them are laughed off, but a lot of them stick.

What's cockeyed is that you can show twenty sluggings a day on TV, and Mickey Spillane guys knifing and raping, and guys and dames in long hot clinches, but try and have a little good clean fun with sex and brother, you've had it. The church will be breathing down the phone and the network's neck, and mothers' groups will yelp about their kids. You can't have any fun with the basic urge.

Want any more sacred cows? All right, take maids. You can't have a screwy maid in a sketch, unless you want a squawk from some spokesman for domestic workers. Same for all other labor types. Put in a gag about some guy—painter, plasterer, you name it—who gets paid for doing nothing—and the unions'll kill it. You can't have fun with Labor, or Business, or Bankers, or—hell, I can't even count the cows.

Oh sure, there are some legitimate targets. You can always get a laugh out of teachers and artists and poets and diplomats (scientists are out now), and, naturally, crooks. And gags about the "Uppah Clahsses" will always get by. There aren't enough of them left to work up a pressure group. And you can make White Protestants with no visible profession as screwy as you want. All situation comedies are built around White Protestants who don't work. Jackie Gleason got away with being a busdriver, and Desi Arnaz is in show business, but that's about as far as you can go. The only American you can satirize is yourself, and that doesn't hold out for twenty-six weeks.

So that's what's happened to the country that produced Mark Twain and Will Rogers before we all got scared of everything and guys like the Junior Senator came along to shut our mouths up.

So that's it. And you've got more to lose than I have. You're killing the goose that lays the golden egg. The goose is the tradition of humor, which is a form of criticism. And you'll never get good comics without it.

2

THE BIG PRETENSIONS

I suppose it has always been difficult and very often dangerous to try to define artistic or creative standards. Now it is certain to evoke violent abuse from those who write or paint or compose by standards which they can define only among themselves in a private calligraphy of their own.

Aware, then, of the outrage destined to greet the following attempts at clarification, I will claim the standards as mine alone and describe the ground from which they grew, laying myself open to whatever charges of age or conservatism or blindness may be used to excuse them.

Until the last war I spent a great part of my life among painters and paintings. My parents took me from the age of eight to the world's great galleries and museums, my school gave me three years of history of art, from Egypt to the French impressionists, my painter friends educated me by the wide range of their respective work, from realist to surrealist to abstract, and I myself worked for over five years with fair proficiency in the field of portrait sculpture. I cannot imagine living without painting or sculpture: half the pleasures of the world come through my eyes.

If this does not make me an expert, neither does it make me an illiterate in art. And if my increasing absorption in words during the last decades has diminished my contact with artists and the climate of painting, I continue to see their work in museums and galleries and the homes of my friends, and to read from time to time the evaluations of critics. I have, I think, a broad—if not precise—idea of what is going on. And although some of it engages both my attention and my admiration, much of it disturbs me deeply. In terms of today, I cannot dig the leading abstract-expressionists. Or perhaps, I dig them all to well and do not like what I find.

I wish, first, that there were some way to talk about art without ever using the words "modern" or "abstract." Both are in a sense meaningless. A seventeenth-century painting can be "modern" because the living eye finds it fresh and new. A "modern" painting can be outdated because it was a product of the moment and not of time. As for abstract, nature itself is abstract. Space, form, line, volume—all these are abstract. And there can be more real abstraction in a Corot landscape, for instance, than in the bleak scribbles of some contemporary artist.

Whether they are accurate or not, however, modern and abstract have come to mean to most people the kind of art in which they cannot recognize the life they know or the emotions they feel. If a painting or a sculpture does not have this recognized content—however illusively or elliptically caught—their instinctive reaction is to find it either repellent, chaotic, disturbing, or simply absurd.

I believe this is true of the majority of people today. Opposing them are a strong, convinced aggressive and vocal minority who either produce "abstract" art, write about it, or prefer it to all other forms of visual experience. I wish I could cast my lot with this minority, not because it is one, but because I believe in the periodic need for revolution as well as the continuing need for evolution, in the creative instinct for experimentation, in the ever-widening boundaries of our perception. Since the present contains within it the future as well as the past, it is the poor artist who does not project himself forward in time as well as backward in accumulated knowledge. No painter with a deep drive can be content with painting snow scenes with blue shadows or Thanksgiving with Grandma, however ably or remuneratively. No sculptor of value will turn out an infinite succession of dancing dryads or boys on dolphins. If they do, they have stopped seeing and feeling, and are merely reproducing popular stereotypes of accepted older forms. I find this kind of art as sterile as I find a great proportion of the abstractions produced today, and totally lacking in the vitality which good abstract art possesses.

I have, furthermore, no desire to join the great chorus of derision at any form of artistic expression not immediately understood or palatable. People who say, "I can't stand modern art" usually know little of any art. And although the "my five-year-old could do better than that" art-lover has been considerably fortified by the excellent abstractions produced by apes, he is—in the last analysis —not far from a tree himself. These are the people responsible for the fact that we have the worst public monuments of any country and make the least use of good contemporary art for the beauty of our buildings and cities. And yet, in a sense, the primary fault lies in the artist who has abstracted himself too far from the rest of his fellows, who no longer is either desirous or capable of communicating with them. With his arrogance, his enclosure, his rejection of all common symbols, he has spoiled the market for the serious and humble painters who are trying to convey the world about them in new terms of vision. And before we go any further I would like to introduce to you one of his kind: a painter called Norman.

Soul for sale

For centuries the eyes of the artist were turned outward on the world about him. What he painted was, to be sure, as much an image of himself as of what he saw, since all creation is a reflection of the creator. But still he observed with humility the external miracle of nature, deriving from it and imposing upon it his own vision thereof.

But lately, painters like Norman have turned their vision inward. Ignoring what is about them, they concentrate with humility on what is inside them. What they see there is then recorded in paint, unframed, and—to a surprising extent—sold.

Norman sees explosions. His paintings, seldom less than six feet square, are a series of disintegrations in violent colors: orange fragments splintered on a thick white field, scarlet clusters, or even black vortices. As in his earlier phase of tempestuous scratchings, the pigment is very thick, the intent very sure. There is no question that he is putting down what he wants to put down: himself.

Two decades ago, Norman's pictures would have shocked the ordinary public, eliciting ridicule and the well-used dictum, "My five-year-old could do better than that." Now people are numbed. They stand in silence before his paintings. Critics have made them feel inadequate, stuffy and blind. Unhappily they search for meanings they have been told reside in the framed spatterings, bewildered they wait for the emotional experience that is promised them. Was it not only yesterday that one well-known critic wrote of Norman that he was "groping with increasing assurance through the developing layers of plastic consciousness" and another that "He has evolved from his earlier linear conflicts into a masterful control of spatial entities"? Don't his larger paintings sell for two thousand dollars, and weren't two of them bought by museums?

The answer is a resounding "Yes." Norman has a strong partisan public who claim him as one of America's most promising painters, a dedicated explorer of the nonobjective world. Norman, they say, has cast off the moldy garments of realism. His painting is the pure act of creation—the moment itself, let us say, of fission.

Norman does not look either fissioned or nonobjective. He is a pleasant-looking young man with regular features and a taut figure, and his only eccentricities are a close-cropped head and a habit of wearing sneakers and blue jeans on all occasions. His air of barefoot boy probably won him his first and most faithful sponsor, a middle-aged widow of wealth whose home is lined with bright eruptions.

Let none mistake it: Norman works much harder than your five-year-old. Nothing is harder to pin down than chaos. Sometimes it takes Norman a whole month to paint a canvas like "Counter-tensions"—a splintering of grays on a yellow field that some foolish woman said "would make a lovely screen." Norman is used to Philistines; they are always with us.

Yet, oddly enough, this woman was not a Philistine. She recognized Norman's real talents, which are for color and for a kind of impulsive patterning that could indeed be used attractively in rugs or hangings or—God save poor Norman—chintzes. Believing that decoration was primarily design without content, she recognized in Norman's painting the presence of the first and the absence of the second.

But, as you say, is not Norman painting his vision of himself? Is that not content? What more do you ask than the examination of the creative soul? You ask, possibly, that the soul be truly creative. You ask whether the expression of self is a creative act if that self is as confused, immature, untrained and intolerant as Norman's.

For Norman is a young man who rejects the past, hides from the present, and ignores the future. He does all this by a total preoccupation with self, an object so compelling that he has never seen beyond it to the shape of a leaf, the curve of a woman's neck, the feathering of cirrus.

To whom is this soul of Norman attractive? What sort of people admire, buy, and live with his explosions? Well, there are the priestesses of the nonobjective cult, intense and dedicated, who have abandoned the banal, "natural" world for the angular white temples of their homes and conversation that is a litany of abstractions. There are the angrily rebellious young who share Norman's impatience with the past and get a bang from the shock waves of his color. There are the men and women who think they see in his jigsaws their own fragmented souls. And there are of course the critics and the dealers, who know that in a time when people are not sure what they want or believe, paintings like Norman's can be praised and sold.

If you think that the critical double-talk which sells a painter like Norman to the public is exaggerated, here is an actual preface from the catalogue of an exhibition in a fashionable gallery of abstract-expressionist art: (there are dozens like this each year): "The morphology of art— reconsidering its philosophical bases—has abandoned in total indifference the three-dimensional form, wasted now by supersaturation, in favor of flat planes of spatial structures. This has resulted in a growing development of the psychosensual aspect of aesthetic appreciation of the onlooker."

The paintings referred to did indeed show a total indifference to three dimensional form, and were—like Norman's—huge. The paint was spilled, dribbled, slapped, spattered, running and clotted; the triumph of accident over plan. This dependence on size and accident was explained once in a distinguished magazine of art as follows:

"The Abstract-Expressionists . . . made it a practice of painting big almost all of the time. Some of their techniques (like Pollock's dripped enamel) could best be exploited over large areas. . . . More important, the artist at work on a big canvas found he was enveloped by it. . . . He could 'Paint himself into the picture. . . .'

"It [the bigness] increases the *intimacy* between the painter and his work. Little thought is given, as there was by older painters, of intimacy between the picture and the spectator." So much for the spectator.

"Facility of drawing an observed or imagined object," wrote the same critic, "is the traditional way in which an artist's first talent is recognized. . . . But avant-garde New York abstractionists, looking for the most immediate methods possible, ruled out drawing as a stage of planning that would inhibit the free flow of sensation between act and object." So much for craftmanship.

For craftmanship is a dirty word in this language, an inhibitor of vision and feeling. And this fact alone, I think, counts for the major weakness in abstract-expressionism as a form of painting: although its better practitioners may possess traditional disciplines, it can be achieved without them. Just as contemporary literature is full of bad writers who can still convey "free flows of sensation" in the manner of a Kerouac, abstract-expressionism is a haven for bad painters free to make accident virtue.

The best possible service that could be done for a bewildered and often deceived public, then, is to tell them how to separate the sheep from the goats on the primary basis of craftmanship rather than content, for no matter what is painted or sculptured, evidence of care, of skill, of knowledge of the medium is there to be recognized. I doubt if anyone who responds to the sensory pleasures of form and surface which only skill can evoke will fail to recognize it in a Brancusi or a Henry Moore or a Lipshitz, even though he may prefer more familiar "subjects." And although some may still find Braque too

abstract or Klee too strange or Mondrian too clinically se-
vere, the enormous care involved in their work is trans-
parently clear.

And so, among the less widely known artists now, there
are painters who express themselves wholly in flat areas,
plane against plane, tone against tone, with no concession
to outward realities, but you can see the tenderness and
concern with which they oppose these planes and colors,
and with which the paint itself is laid on. There are
painters who only indicate, in the most tenuous impres-
sionistic manner, their perceptions of the world, but there
is skill and control in their very tenuosity. There are
strong and virile abstractionists whose forms and colors
sing like a brass band, direct and certain, and this needs
skill. And there are wholly abstract sculptors—manipula-
tors of space—who can create out of a geometry of wire an
aesthetic experience; like, for instance, the magnificent
golden sun of Richard Lippold.

I am not speaking of these but of the others who dominate the abstract scene, the painters of "pure sensation,"
the primitives, the private and arrogant communicators
with self. I see in their painting another form of delinquency, a revolt against form and order, against reason
itself. It represents only one segment of contemporary art,
but it is given a prestige and attention far beyond its
worth in artistic, if not in social, terms.

Beyond all these manifestations, good and bad, of new
aesthetic approaches, I am constantly amazed at the assumption that there is nothing left in the physical, external, world worth conveying in form or pigment: the
premise that the camera has usurped entirely the role of
observation and recognition, and that henceforth the artist must disassociate—"free"—himself from such concrete

dimensions. But science has brought new physical dimensions which most artists ignore. What of the magnificent patterns and contours of earth as seen in flight, or the massive and complex conformations of weather in the sky? What of the new world in the lens of the microscope and the telescope? Of the world under water? What shapes could be more abstract than these? No camera can convey the emotional experience of these new dimensions as well as the insight of the artist could. And what of the more familiar but still mysterious forms of the single leaf, the sea-abraded stone, the shell, the feather, a cluster of twigs, the eroded ridges of rock? Is there nothing more to see in them, no new way of sharing them? I doubt it. The world of sight is still limitless. It is the artist who limits vision to the cramped dimensions of his own ego.

From the covers of the *Saturday Evening Post* to the pathological explosions of bad abstractionists, there is a universe of sight. If critics and exhibitors and curators have any function, it is to encourage painters to communicate it and the public to experience it; to give people timeless aesthetic standards by which to measure the values of the art they see; and to stop the double-talk, the preposterous jargon of the abstractionist world, which is nothing more than an abdication of judgment and an invitation to artistic chicanery. The public has been sold a bill of goods long enough.

In speaking of art—and this time I mean music and poetry and dance as well as painting and sculpture—the word "beauty" is no longer admissible today because no one can define it. The prevailing concept is that since adjectives like "beautiful" and "ugly" are entirely subjective, varying in an infinite number of degrees with each single beholder, they are meaningless. Certainly I will not attempt here to say what beauty is.

Yet I will, at the risk of using other unfashionable and discarded words, tell what a work of art should do and what a work which is not art fails to do. And this is, quite simply, to make the beholder a better human being; nobler, larger, purer, and more perceptive. Art can excite, titillate, please, entertain, and sometimes shock; but its ultimate function is to ennoble. Surely the hold of great music on the listener is precisely this: that the listener is made whole; and at the same time part of an image of infinite grace and grandeur which is creation.

I know, for myself, that this is so. And that the times when this pattern becomes clearest and when I aspire highest in terms of compassion and understanding are those moments when I have listened to passages of Palestrina or Bach or Mozart or Brahms or Beethoven. Nor do only such major expressions produce a state of grace and enlargement. A song, a lyric, a line of poetry, a sentence can do it. So, in art, can the simplest drawing or a painting one foot square. Size, or importance of content, have nothing to do with it. The intent of the creator has everything to do with it.

This is why I find so much contemporary music and painting and poetry so inadequate. It is singularly without nobility, because it is concerned more with the act than with the aim, with the means than with the end. There is a great aridity in the swaggering areas of canvas and the long niggling parade of notes and sounds that pass for compositions. They are suffused with the monotony of nihilism, that kingdom of sensation without meaning that some mistake for art. Certainly they leave the observer and the listener no better than he was, and possibly worse; restless and disturbed, as if he had been listening at length to someone with an impediment of speech. Like their plebeian relative, "Rock and Roll," their insistence is neurotic and sets up a chain-reaction that breaks down rather than builds up: fission again, instead of fusion.

It is exaggerated, of course, to cite Rock and Roll as a "cause" of delinquency. But it may not be exaggerated to suspect that in its manic monotony it is an agent of destruction, breaking down the few feeble controls that still hold the young in balance. The popular and folk music of other times do not do this. They are repetitious but not manic; their beat is the natural beat of the heart and not the trigger-stutter of a hop-head. There is, finally, an impurity about these contemporary expressions that expresses a deeper pollution. You see it in the faces of young and old, you hear it in foul language, you breathe it in desecrated air. It is a loss of innocence; a quite wilful loss, as if it were unmanly to retain it. And the odd thing is that you cannot throw words like heroism and sacrifice and nobility and honor away without abandoning the qualities they express. Any more than you can guarantee the retention of freedom and democracy merely by constant iteration of the words alone. Form and content are not separable.

And beauty? Except in women, we have thought so little of it for so long that we have produced one of the ugliest civilizations in the world wherever nature has been invaded. Maybe the time has come now to redefine it and reinstate its worth. One small oblique attempt in the realm of music follows.

Dissonant dialogue

They were sitting around, eight of them, listening to records of contemporary music. One was a composer, one a pianist, two a man and wife dedicated to the support of modern American music, one a teacher of composition, two students, and a woman with a troubled look. When the last record had ended and there was a pause punctuated by low murmurs of appreciation, she said, "Do you think we could play a little Mozart now?"

They turned to look at her, jarred.

"Still unconverted?" said the pianist, smiling.

"Don't worry about Mary," said the patron-host. "She just likes to graze in old pastures."

"I don't know if I care for that image," said the woman, "but frankly, I don't think I can take any more of what we've been hearing."

"What do *you* think we've been hearing?" asked the teacher.

"Wanderings," said the woman, "interminable wanderings in sound, interrupted now and then by excursions into noise."

"How about a drink, everybody?" said the hostess cheerily, rising. "What'll you have?"

The rest gave their orders and split into intense little analytical groups. The woman was left alone—exiled, she felt—with her trouble, until the composer came over and sat next to her.

"It's strange," he said, "how liberals can be so conservative about music." He went on to speak about a certain music critic on a magazine that espoused liberal causes who was consistently inhospitable to most modern music, especially American.

"I think that's a weak generalization," said the woman. "It's no more true than to say that reactionaries love modern music. But if you're going to include me in this blanket charge, I think I can come up with at least one explanation of the paradox."

The composer looked at her expectantly, genuinely curious as to why such a block (his definition of her attitude toward modern music) could exist in one of her intelligence.

"The active liberal," she said, "lives in an atmosphere of flux and tension and doubt. There is much chaos and little pattern in the political world. It is atonal, dissonant, explosive. Because of this he craves order and harmony in art. After a day of headlines he needs Bach, not Sessions. In an age of constant change, he needs classic reaffirmations of constant values. In an age of violence, he profoundly desires peace. Surely whatever other qualities modern music may have, peace is not one of them."

"I think you're confusing peace with cessation," said the composer. "Status quo. And as for form or pattern, do you honestly believe that because you do not find it in Sessions or Krenek it does not exist? Do I have to bring up

that old chestnut about artists misunderstood and vili-
fied in their time now being popular and crystal clear—
like, say, Stravinsky?"

"He may be clear as crystal," she said, "and I admire
him very much. But I still maintain that after a day of
Dulles or Khrushchev I am much less inclined to put 'The
Rites of Spring' on the record player than 'Don Giovanni.'

"If you must know," she continued, almost visibly buck-
ling on her armor, "the one common quality I find in most
modern music—and I am talking only about the 'abstract'
composers, not men like Barber or Copland or Menotti or
Dello Joio—is that it is disruptive and disturbing."

"You mean it makes you think, it shakes you out of your
cozy familiar preoccupation with Bach, Beethoven,
Brahms?"

The woman remarked that most modern music did not
make her think of anything except the composer's poverty
of soul and the end of his piece, should that ever arrive.
She said that if she suspected talent running through his
incoherence, she was angry because of the effort involved
in discovering it. If there was no talent—merely a preten-
tious use of the most rigid modern idiom—she was even
angrier.

"In other words, you find it disturbing because you simply do not understand it."

"If so," she said, "I am in a formidable majority—a
much greater majority than those who still flinch at Pi-
cassos and Légers. *Your* audience," she said, "consists of a
dedicated band of modern music practitioners and lovers,
augmented by a slightly larger band of people who find it
fashionable to pretend they understand it."

"In the absence of Gallup polls on the subject," said the
composer, with an edge to his voice, "I can only say that

this majority of yours must be obtuser than I thought."
The woman, calm until now, exploded. "There we go
again! The calm assumption by avant-garde painters and
composers and poets that people must learn *their* language—never that *they* must first learn to speak to people!
This is the supreme arrogance of the Private 'I': 'Here is
my cipher, boys, come and decode it.' I used to believe
that art was a form of communcation."

The composer tried to be patient. "Just what do you expect a young composer writing today to do—turn out little
copies of Schubert and Chopin? What can he do but reflect the world he lives in!"

"Reflect?" she said. "Not exactly. I think I expect any
artist to do two things: accept the past and fuse the
present. If there is chaos, it is up to him not merely to
reflect it but to give it meaning and shape; or rather, to
find the central core momentarily obscured by chaos. The
sky, for instance, may be a raging vortex of clouds, but the
structure of the universe remains unchanged."

"Forget the vortex," said the composer, "and concentrate on the pretty little stars."

"You can hardly accuse the great classic composers,"
she protested, "of avoiding the vortex. If anyone has trans-
lated deeper passions and greater conflicts into sound
than Brahms and Beethoven and Bach, I would like to
hear him."

"What you are really saying, you know, is that there
should be no change in musical form or expression from
the Three B's."

"Certainly there should. But not just because they are
new or different. If a man doesn't know what he wants to
say, or has nothing to say, no chorus of typewriters, dinner gongs, steam drills, and squash gourds is going to

help him. Neither is a beat alien to the basic human rhythm."

"I don't know what you're talking about," said the composer. "What would you call the basic human rhythm?"

The woman paused for a moment, searching for clarity. "Well, the beat of the heart, the rhythm of breathing. There they are, in everyone; definite, regular, inevitable. This beat, this breathing, must have its echo in music."

"Dum-de-dum-de-dum-de-dum," said the composer, scornfully.

"Don't be silly. Why are great melodies never forgotten? Because they take flight on the wings of breath. They are, literally and figuratively, man's aspiration. It's the same with great poetry; it has the cadence of the heart. But take so much of contemporary music, modern music. It is a pant, a stutter, a stammer. The nearest image I can relate to it is the walk of a spastic. You people seem to have some sort of disease of the soul. Your progression in music is one of fits and starts; it stumbles and wavers, gibbering as it goes. And even when it has a clear direction, it is so often one of assault—a series of jabs and punches designed to shock the ear into attention."

"Pretty images," said the composer, grinning. "You must come and hear my latest composition some day!"

The woman smiled too. "Thanks. I am always open to a new experience, even if I don't like it when I have it."

At the opposite end of the cultural spectrum from Mary and her Mozart, a lover of peace and order and purity, is the young person, male or female, who rejects them fiercely, finding them a prison of old forms from which they must, at all costs, free themselves. Norman, our fictional painter, was one of them, but they populate all the arts; and you will find them in any public place where a new poem is read, a new jazzman heard, a new composition played, or a Beckett work performed. Intense, disheveled, and often unmannerly, they have the look of somnambulists, walking and thinking in their sleep, drugged with sensation and isolated from reality. Some of them have talent, some of them have none, but they all share a contempt for the past, assured that it has no relevance to their future. Rejecting the concept of continuity, they live for the moment, and for themselves, like nearly all who are young. But the rejection and enclosure of these particular young is the more emphatic because of the bland patterns of the society around them. They have to struggle harder than we did to be themselves, and there is another difference, I think, besides. At their age, we wanted to be different and better. They are quite content to be different. And the joke is that, clinging to difference, they cleave to conventions and patterns even more rigid, if far less bland, than those of the larger society they reject.

Here is one little refugee who has changed prisons; not typical, perhaps, but perhaps recognizable.

Dance-lover

You will find her at any evening of ballet and at most dance recitals. Her name is Lee, and she wears her thick, long, straight brown hair pulled back into a horsetail with elastic bands.

You will also recognize her by her sturdy, short, muscular body and by the amount of crude leather she displays on her person—a wide calf belt with coins set in it, a shoulder bag like a horse's feedbag, and sandals with a great many straps. In these her feet are planted almost defiantly.

She wears very full skirts that are too long, and very tight jerseys that display an aggressive bust. Her face is full-lipped and intense.

Lee is very passionate about dancing. It is her life. When she is not actually bending and stretching and leaping and squatting, she is looking at others leap and squat. When she is not looking, she is thinking of dancing, reading of dancing, dreaming of dancing.

This does not mean that she admires all kinds of dancing. Although conceding a certain technical proficiency, Lee finds classical ballet reactionary and frivolous. It is pretty (abhorrent quality) and means nothing. To Lee, everything must *mean something*. The more tragic the meaning, the higher the art. That is why Lee is such a violent partisan of the abstract approach. There is not a movement of the body that does not mean something, usually of a pretty desperate nature.

Lee knows that the dance is far more than a bodily function. To be any good, it must spring from a richly cultivated mental and emotional soil. Lee's soil is composed of Kafka, Sartre, the *Evergreen Review* and Jackson Pollock. The plot is wide enough to include Hieronymus Bosch and Henry Miller, but then the fence begins. In Lee's mind nothing created before 1900 is of any interest (except Bosch), and nothing lucid is of any importance. Only complexity has meaning. So when Lee recognizes an object in a painting, that damns the painter; and when she understands a line in a poem, that poet is representational and therefore lousy. As obscurity is a cherished quality in much of art, Lee is a happy girl.

In contrast to this, her moral concepts are surprisingly out of date. She believes in untrammeled sex as a free expression of personality. Lee dismisses monogamy as a delusion. She alarms most of the young men she knows with repeated hints at producing a baby. Illegitimately, of course. There would be no point in a legitimate one.

Next to embarrassing men, Lee finds deep enjoyment in embarrassing the government. This takes the form of agitating for immediate action when the government is either incapable of taking it or engaged in delicate maneuvers to avoid it. The action would be fatal, but Lee is for it. She is currently picketing the consulate of an ally for motives which bear no relation to the actual facts but which bear every relation to Lee's emotions.

Like the Russians, Lee has a vocabulary all her own. It goes something like this: Authority=dictatorship. Diplomat=fool. Patience=cowardice. Wisdom=inertia. Breeding=snobbishness. Charm=hypocrisy. The past=reaction. Anyone Who Lives Comfortably=a reactionary.

These definitions have one common denominator: innocence. Lee has never known authority; never met a diplomat; never had patience; lacks wisdom; possesses no breeding; exerts no charm; is ignorant of the past; and lives uncomfortably.

In spite of this, Lee will probably develop into a very good dancer, of the school which defies the essence of the dance by never leaving the ground. As her center of gravity is very low, this is all for the best.

3

ARBITERS OF TASTE

To be successful in the world of art you must, of course, have talent, although very small talents have gone very far in this age. Just as the microphone gave volume to voices that had none, so does the science of press-agentry magnify limited skills into highly saleable properties. Evidence of this abounds in the movies where a stupid girl with stupefying dimensions can become a star, and on television, where a nice-looking boy with a pleasant voice can become an idol.

But to be a success in the world of fine arts is not quite so simple or so direct. The talent is more important here, but it is by no means enough. What is needed is the acceptance and support of a relatively small group of men and women who both dominate and coordinate the centers of criticism and fashion, or I might say, the fashions of criticism. And while an Arthur Miller or a Gian Carlo Menotti or a Robert Frost can reach the public heart without their help, it is virtually impossible for those of lesser talent to gain wide acceptance without them.

Who are they? Well, some of them are men and women of integrity and perception who review the arts for our best newspapers and more serious magazines. Some of them are wealthy hostesses with cultural inclinations or artistic pretensions who "take up" a writer or composer or painter and see that he meets the people useful to him. But many belong to a very special group, in New York at least (and I am sure this is so in London and Paris as well), who are on the periphery of art and of life and who achieve their power through one major and common talent: a sense of fashion. Fashion in clothes, fashion in decor, fashion in place, and fashion in thought. They have unerring noses for the right time and the right people, and their definition of "right" is, of course, successful.

It is this charmed and potent circle that I now enter here:

The women who visit Robin's apartment are inclined to wonder why men ever bother to marry: They live so much more comfortably alone. And indeed, Robin's place is perfection—a garden duplex in New York's East Sixties furnished in exquisite taste in a mixture of Regency and modern, run by a pale and graceful Negro, animated by a huge and uncannily sensitive brown poodle, and free of such blurring traces of feminine presence as stockings drying in the bathroom and a clutter of jars. Even the canapés are better than the ones in the homes of the married.

Robin, moreover, appears to be exempt from those devotions, obligations, and incubi which make other people tired and old and cross, harried, debt-ridden, and dull.

If he has aging parents, they are never seen; being un-married, he has neither children nor parents-in-law; old friends who are dull are friends no more; and even cousins seem not to exist. Since he has no one to support, it is perhaps no wonder that the sums he earns through his thriving business of interior decoration should be spent entirely on himself and on a way of life entirely pleasing to himself. And it must be admitted that Robin is an artist in pleasure, choosing only those objects, colors, sounds, and textures which flatter the senses, excluding those which offend or enervate. The exclamation of delight uttered by a new visitor gives Robin a sense of altruism dispelling any faint twinge (the twinges are fainter every year) of remorse at what some people have called his selfish life. He gives pleasure freely to others; and if they are so transported by his taste as to demand his professional services—well, then, that is their concern. He did not force them into it.

Robin has other attributes besides taste. He is quite decorative, in a fluid way, and very funny. He has a pronounced gift for mimicry, and it is generally felt that he could have adorned the theater.

There is, in fact, no field of creative effort in which Robin is not entirely at home. His cocktail parties and little buffets are likely to include the most successful photographers, painters, choreographers, composers and writers in town, and certainly the leaders in the world of fashion. No fashion editor worth her salt fails to know Robin and count him as her friend, and his decors and the works of his companions are responsible for her most spectacular pages. It might be said indeed that Robin's circle *is* the fashion.

It is a tightly closed society, this circle: a light and airy *cénacle* of the arts; or, if you prefer, an Old Pals' Act rigid in its dedication and loyalty. The larger society is split up into smaller cells: painter, art critic, dealer; composer, music critic, performer; dancer, choreographer, manager; poet, editor, publisher; and so forth. Around these separate cells is a chorus of young men and older women, a galaxy of the rootless, there to applaud, to cosset, to crown. It is the rare artist who succeeds without belonging to Robin's world.

Robin and his companions have many talents but little love, except for these talents and for each other, and theirs is a love that leads inward. They love their love of beauty, they love their sensibilities, and they love their persons. With great attention they keep supple and slim, offering their skin as often as they can to the golden approval of the sun. For this purpose, they claim the best beaches and the best coasts in the world, from Fire Island to Barbados, from Morocco to Corsica. And when these beaches are ultimately found and claimed by the vulgar, or spoiled by wars, they move to others more distant, more concealed. Stumble upon a beautiful hidden cove and Robin will be there sunning, his russet or mahogany towel beside him, his bright hair cropped on his skull, and the poodle, Flaubert, bounding at the waves.

Yet the gaiety, the ease and the brilliance that characterize the world of Robin do not preclude a netherworld, one which is darker than one might suppose and inhabited by things that are not pretty. Spite, jealousy, rage, revenge—these are a few of the monsters that plague Robin's society. The energies others expend on supporting wives, raising families, and enduring illness, monotony, or privation are here diverted into intense and exclusive relationships. When these are harmonious, all is perfect. When they sour, hell is unleashed. The one found guilty of the breach becomes quite suddenly the object of bad reviews, for the sweetest ostracism in this circle is professional, and the course of personal relationships can be quite easily followed in the critical press. Over or beneath it all—this exquisite, tasteful, witty, and powerful stratum—is a profound discontent that neither Robin nor his friends ever allow themselves to admit, for they consider themselves in nearly all ways superior to their fellows. They are, for all their success, not in the mainstream of life, for the one quality absent in their world is humanity.

Yet humanity might blur their judgment, might impel them, out of affection or pity, to accept a failure, a talent out of its time, an embarrassment. And this no arbiter of taste can afford to do.

IV

PERSONAL HERESIES

1

SUBJECTIVELY YOURS

Women are repeatedly accused of taking things personally. I cannot see any other honest way of taking them. Only experts can assume objectivity, which is only another word for noncommitment, and I am clearly not an expert. But I am committed to a certain view of the world by nature of my origins, my background and my experience. And if I have spent some time on these here it is because I feel it makes more sense to proceed from the particular to the general than to pretend an impersonality and knowledge which will deceive no one. In writing what is known as "social commentary," I could spare myself the inevitable criticism of experts by bolstering my views with their own quotes and with tables of statistics. I could also take cover under those wonderful little phrases with which journalists abdicate responsibility: "According to recent surveys"—"It is generally conceded that . . ."—"It would seem," and so forth. But I do not like to weasel. I assume full responsibility for what I have said here, cheerfully prepared to concede that in certain instances I may be in error, that I do not know enough about what I am talking, and that others have said it better.

But others are not me. And if what I say has any meaning and value, it is because it is said by an American woman of European heritage and middle years who has lived and worked through the major convulsions of the modern world.

I speak, in short, as a human being. And it is one of the deepest sources of my anger that this simple phrase describes the most evaded revolution of our times: the gradual ascendancy of humanity over sex. We talk of it as the loss of sex. It is really the emergence of the individual. And instead of welcoming it as a great step in the march of our fulfilment, we insist upon fostering our differences, allotting to men and to women roles which limit their human capacities and their understanding of each other. It is wonderful to be a woman and it is wonderful to be a man. It is even more wonderful to be oneself. This, I may say, is an uphill fight. I know, because I have fought it.

"You can do anything," my father used to say when I was a child and throughout my girlhood. "You can be anything you want to be." The outer world set limits, but he did not. The outer world said "dolls, marriage, babies, cooking, dolls." He said, "Keep dreaming." And so I dreamed all my youth of being many things and people, from d'Artagnan to Joan of Arc, from Guinevere to Theseus, from Pavlova to Leonardo, from Scott to Keats. There was no ceiling to imagination, no fence to aspiration. I was simply in love, and still am, with the power and glory of man. I see nothing more grotesque in a woman yearning to be an astronomer than a man yearning to be a dancer. We should be free to do both, and to love each other, and to reproduce this love. But we are not. Most of us are molded by our parents and our society from infancy to conform not merely to the outlines dictated by our biology but to a pattern imposed by men, long dead, for their convenience. It is time that men and women were let alone, to be what they want to be and not what society expects of them. Certainly, as a woman I am profoundly weary of the avalanche of advice for what is called our good: of being chivied by churchmen, sociologists, psychiatrists and experts in all fields to accept a clearly defined role for the preservation of the community. Let us by all means love men and marry them, bear children and love them, cook well and like it; but let that not be an end any more than a man's work is an end, but rather parts of an infinitely larger whole which is membership in the human race.

2

LETTER TO A GIRL

My dear daughter whom I never had,

Perhaps it is just as well that you do not exist because you would have had a tough time with me as a mother. For on top of the normal difficulties of an always complex relationship I would have subjected you to a kind of thinking and feeling which would have put you at odds with the society in which you lived. I might even have pulled you out of this society at a certain age so that you might better be able to build up a resistance to some of its infections. I most certainly would have made you unhappy and lonely at a time when American girls are the queens of the world. Shall I tell you why?

For one thing, I should not start from the cradle assuming that because you were a girl you had only one road in life and one function. For you are not one entity, but several, having masculine qualities as well as feminine, bearing within you the infinite combinations, sexual, intellectual, physical, of past generations. As a child I would provide you with toy cars as well as with dolls, with trains as well as tea sets, for who am I to say that you should not grow to be interested in wheels as well as dia-pers? And when you were old enough to read I would see that your range was complete and not confined to the girlish slop imposed on female children by normal par-ents. If you preferred to read about girls (which I would doubt; boys are more fun), that would be your business. But the choice would be there, and the encouragement to experiment in many areas not confined to your sex.

I would dress you attractively, of course; but I would be far more disturbed at an early clothes-consciousness in yourself than the lack of it. That can come later; much later. I find little girls who are perpetually preening them-selves, swinging little bags, talking about clothes, nothing more than embryo bitches—the calculating, not the hearty, kind. As for the mother who gives a girl-child permanents and lets her wear nail polish, she is perform-ing an act of desecration which is almost obscene.

I would give you all the information on sex you showed yourself ready for by asking it, at any time in your devel-opment. But I would show obvious disgust with the kind of talk of dating and boy friends that starts—in most American families, it seems—at the age of eight and be-comes obsessive by the age of twelve. This is meretricious sex—the kind of thing imposed by the constant barrage of television, radio, movies and magazines aimed indis-criminately at the young as well as the old. I am deeply disturbed by schoolgirls from twelve to sixteen who wear heavy make-up, tint their hair and engineer their breasts. Not only are they coarsened; they miss a time of utmost importance in the life of anyone—the age of innocence. I know I would have trouble in this country keeping you from using make-up until you were fifteen. But I would try—hard. I would also tell you that the longer you stayed away from girdles and bras the better. No healthy young body needs support. Foundations serve only two purposes: to push the body into shapes of current fashion and to substitute (and eventually weaken) the pelvic and pectoral muscles which were meant to support you. The commercial and social pressures on you to wear them would be enormous and probably successful. But I would still tell you: wait until you need them.

Having traveled a great deal in other countries I agree with those who find American girls the most beautiful, the best-dressed and the best-groomed in the world. They are a delight to look at; ample evidence that good food, exercise and a high standard of physical attention can make nearly any girl appetizing, if a little antiseptic. The fashion magazines too have performed their great service in the refinement of feminine taste and the accentuation of beauty wherever it may be found. I would expect you by the time you were sixteen to look at *Vogue* and *Harper's Bazaar* and learn from them.

But I would hope fervently that before this you would have gone through a plain stage where you were neither attracted to or by boys; where you dreamed of life on your own single terms; where you would rather read the legend of King Arthur than go to a school dance; where you imagined yourself anything from Margot Fonteyn to Mrs. Franklin D. Roosevelt. I would want wiser and older men to take an interest in your growing mind. I would want you to paint or learn an instrument or a language, or study ballet-dancing. I would most certainly want you to relish good food and learn how to cook it. More than anything, I would want you to be alone quite a lot. I would even want you to be miserable.

This is because I feel it is the only way you will learn

both your identity and a sense of humility. For I cannot believe that the girls who are "adjusted," boy-crazy, attractive and dated from the age of twelve have time to learn either. They are following a pattern imposed on them since birth; a sort of infantile mating dance which has no core of experience in love and which has as its sole fulfilment a child-marriage.

It is popular now to cast a benign and approving eye on the young folk who go steady, marry at eighteen and start producing at twenty. I view it far from benignly. It is supposed to be evidence of new, sensible, "need for security"; of a young vital race getting down to its major job of increasing an already overpopulated world. Quite often, no doubt, it works out well, although I wonder if adults are produced by children producing children. As for the idea of starting to "go steady" in your adolescence, I call it a preposterous limitation of growth, curiosity, adventure, fun. Poor girl who dances with one boy all evening, every date! How dull! And the only reason it is the accepted pattern now is not tender and touching fidelity but fear of being left alone: the worst, apparently that can befall a girl. Yet I would tell you, on the contrary, that an evening spent alone is infinitely preferable to an evening stuck with a bore. This is the major disaster.

I would hope that you were chaste until you were eighteen. After that I would be much more concerned with your heart than with your chastity. There is a lot of hypocritical nonsense being said about the dire consequences to the female of premarital sexual relations. They are supposed to endanger all hope of future happiness. I can only tell you that it depends entirely on their nature. If you are intimate with a boy, or man, purely out of curiosity or for what *you* can get out of it, sex can be a soiling and spoiling experience. If you love, or really think you love the man, if you want to give *him* love, sex can be an enrichment. Between a girl who gives herself for these reasons and out of a real affection for men, and the girl who withholds herself for purposes of ultimate gain (a wedding ring, i.e., security), I prefer the morality of the former. To me the real bitch is the teaser; the girl who, without any especial affection or desire, uses men for her own ends.

It is a marvelous thing, and something of a miracle, if you find at eighteen the permanent answer to your dreams of love. It is equally marvelous, if you find at any time in your life a man preferable to all others as a life companion. Monogamy is a condition devoutly to be desired, and earnestly to be striven for. But from my own observation, the women who have achieved it most successfully are very often the women who have loved a number of men and learned the difficult but rewarding art of living with them. Give me the generous woman every time. Certainly the bane of men's existence is the ungenerous one.

All this, of course, is rankest heresy. But it seems to me the only honest approach in a day when fear of pregnancy is no longer a deterrent to sexual intimacy among the young and when—in spite of a thousand sermons on virtue—the young are incited to sex by everything they see, read and hear. Equally dishonest—and from the point of view of society, dangerous—is the religious pressure against birth control when it is not only practiced by all civilized peoples but essential to all primitive ones. I am sickened by the arguments that if a child is born blind of a syphilitic mother and a degenerate father, it is God's will. Whose God?

So you see, my dear daughter who never was, you would have a rough time if you lived today unless, unlike your mother, you kept all these attitudes to yourself. But if you did, you would not be my daughter—would you?

3

IF I WERE A MAN

If I were a man, I'd be a rake until I married; and that, with any luck, would not be till my late twenties. I cannot imagine a better occupation of spare time than the seduction of a number of different women—unless, if you are a woman, it is seduction by a number of different men. It depends on what you are. It depends on how much vitality you have. It depends, certainly, on how fond you are of the opposite sex. And I find the theory—propounded daily and lengthily by the ladies who write columns of advice in the papers—that this kind of sport is a sign of immaturity in men and disturbance in women—rather preposterous. It may comfort women by diminishing men and elevating themselves, but it is not very convincing. A great many mature, productive and distinguished men have trod the primrose path and a great many wise and productive women have, in their time, tasted the delights of compliance. And how indeed, is one equipped to recognize and practice virtue if one has not experienced its absence? Of what good is control if one has not endured the consequences of its lack?

But the Church and psychiatry have done their best to discredit dilatory passions, with the result that most American men have a very limited understanding of the nature of women, and most American women have suffered from this ignorance. The domesticated male may be safe, but he is not exciting. Nor is a society in which amorous exchanges (usually between persons long married to others) can be initiated only through the release of drink and pursued only behind the country-club hedge. Ten to one that the men and women involved married the girl and boy next door in their teens. This is hardly an education.

For I think this education of men by women and women by men is an essential one. It can happen best through a fortunate marriage, but then again a marriage can be fortunate because both husband and wife have been thus educated and know the nature of love fully. There is nothing more complicated than the long-term relationship between a man and woman, and if I were a man I'd want to look around pretty extensively before I tackled one.

For it is ignorance as well as drink that makes Bill H. think that Susie Q. is a dream-girl and a volcano, while Mary H., pressed close to Harry Q. on the dance-floor, imagines him, deliriously, as a satyr. They are, simply, other people's wives and husbands, usually no better and no worse, no hotter or colder, than the original partner. But the Q.'s and the H.'s had no chance to find this out in their youth. What they are doing now is merely delayed exploration at a time when discovery could be destructive.

That is why I would explore the infinite variety of women before my marriage, rather than after. And I would prefer as my life partner a woman who knew almost as much as I did. I say almost, because I imagine it is in the nature of man to enjoy teaching.

Being a woman, and like all women responding strongly to words, I am continually amazed that so many men do not know the power they can exert through words alone. The attraction of the strong silent lover is a myth, propagated, one might suppose, by inarticulate men. But all really great lovers are articulate, and verbal seduction is the surest road to actual seduction. The man who knows this can be ugly as sin and still prevail over a handsomer tongue-tied rival. Young men can afford to be speechless blunderers, but if they want to exert attraction in later years, they had better learn to talk.

And I do not mean garrulity. I mean talk directly addressed to the woman *about* the woman. Verbal attention is as important as sexual attention. It is the knowledge of what to say, when.

It is also the knowledge of every facet of the woman herself, which must be reflected back to her in words. For the woman—to love a man—must be in love with herself as *he* sees her. This is, of course, a matter of mutual narcissism, but I think it is stronger in women than in men, and more demanding. In any case, I would take great pleasure in presenting this image as accurately to her as I could. General compliments are pleasing to hear, but the specific compliment bears far greater fruit. For the man who remarks on the line of her chin or the shape of her thigh, a woman will do anything.

Having won a woman, I think I would be tough with her; making my dominance of her in the sexual realm quite clear, exacting deference to my masculinity and rebuffing aggressive inroads of all kinds. I would not tolerate the loud or derisive voice or any efforts, private or public, to diminish my stature as a man. I would exert this dominance because women expect and want it; and when they don't get it, they are left with contempt for the man. If American men realized this, they would no longer endure their submissive state, and American women would at least be permitted to enjoy what a wise old artist once called "the voluptuousness of obedience."

If I were a man, I would be a hellion, I would; the kind of man a woman like myself would fall in love with—and probably live to regret it!

4

"OUR WOMEN ARE WONDERFUL," THE AMERICAN SAID SADLY

"I don't know why," said one delegate to another over lunch, "there is all this fuss about American women. I think they are the most wonderful women in the world."

"I'm glad you think so," said the other delegate, who was an American.

"There is always this criticism," the foreigner went on. "They are cold, they are selfish, they are spoiled, they are this and that. Let me tell you something about *our* women."

The American listened attentively.

"Our women can be only one thing at a time. If they are beauties, they spend their lives being beauties. If they are housewives, that is all they do. If they are intellectuals, they are ugly. If they are rich, they are lazy. If they are poor, they are sad. If they are seductive, they are not anything else. If they aren't seductive, they are social workers. But, ah, my friend, one American woman can be everything! I see what a really free society can do for a woman. It is unique."

"I agree with you," said the American. "I married one. Our women are wonderful."

"Ah, your wife," said the foreigner. "So beautiful, so talented, so kind."

"She is all of those things," said the American. "And more."

"You say that so sadly, dear fellow. But why?"

"Because no man," said the American, "can live up to that. Because American women are not only our equals. They have become our superiors."

"Nonsense," said the foreigner, without much conviction.

"But it is true. We have lost our ascendancy. Or rather, we have laid it voluntarily at their feet. My God!" said the American, warming up. "Look around you in any restaurant. What do you see? Beautiful, well-groomed, vivacious, healthy women—with homely, badly dressed, tired men."

"You had the handsomest army in the world, dear fellow."

"Ah, yes, the young men. Before they abdicate."

"But why do you abdicate?"

The American shrugged. "Because it is easier that way. Because we are too busy or too tired to impose our will on our women. Why should we, anyway? They are wiser."

The foreigner shook his head. "That is wrong—very wrong. The man must be the leader. It is natural law. It is the only way the human equation can work."

"But it does not produce the American woman—of whom you think so highly. She would never be what she is if she were dominated by her man. It is her very freedom that has made her all those things you see and admire. She has become a whole human being, not a sort of appendage to a man."

"She is still not a man," said the foreign delegate. "Even

if she invades your offices and your tennis courts and your law courts—you still have your private empire."

"It is a dwindling one," said the American, "reduced to a few weekend hours when the children are not around."

"Because, my dear fellow, you are always in a hurry," said the foreigner, "and then, you never go home for lunch. It is a big mistake. There is nothing that so unifies the sexes as a leisurely lunch with wine, followed by a siesta."

The American laughed. "You can imagine how much work would get done in the afternoon. And besides, one's wife would be out—at a committee luncheon or something."

The foreigner cocked his head to one side quizzically as he looked at his colleague. "May I say something more about these magnificent women of yours—and about yourselves?"

"Go ahead."

"It seems to me that there is a strong analogy in the relation of the American public to their government and the American woman to her man."

The American delegate waited.

"I believe," said the foreigner, "that both your public and your women want leadership and that your government and your men are afraid to give it."

"Or incapable?" the American suggested.

"I don't think so. Merely afraid. Afraid of losing votes. Afraid of losing popularity. Look at your delegation here. Why do they seem so diffident? It's as if they always had one ear nervously cocked for the reaction from home. This fear, my dear man, is losing you both your leadership and your women."

"The alternative is a dictatorship."

"Ah no, ah no!" protested the foreigner vehemently. "You must not confuse leadership with dictatorship. To lead is to show the way."

"There is a fine line there—a dangerous one."

"Not in your country," said the other delegate, "and not with your women. The people make their leaders."

"And the women make their men?" asked the American. "Isn't that an admission that both the American people and the American women do not want to be led?"

"No. It is only an admission that you—you American men—do not want to lead. And that is a tragedy."

Both men looked at the clock and rose. As they parted, the American said, "Tell me, if you were not already married, would you marry an American woman?"

"Heaven forbid!" said the foreigner.

5

THE CASE OF THE TWO-HEADED WOMAN

The following is a transcript of an imaginary television interview between a Professional Prober and me:

PP: Miss Mannes, you would call yourself a career woman, would you not?
MM: *I* wouldn't. But other people might.
PP: I take it that you object to the term?
MM: Well, it still has an edge of distaste. It conjures up the kind of militant and aggressive woman who has shouldered her way into a man's world at the expense of her femininity—her real functions.
PP: What are a woman's real functions?
MM: Don't you know?
PP: (*with an embarassed laugh*) I am asking *you* what you think they are.
MM: I can tell you what they are supposed to be: wifehood and motherhood.
PP: Do you take issue with that?
MM: Only in degree. We were made to live with men and

have children and rear them, but I think there is more to a woman than that.

PP: You mean, it isn't enough for a woman to be a good wife and a good mother?

MM: It's enough for a great many women, and I envy them their completion. But it isn't enough for myself.

PP: Why do you envy these women?

MM: Because theirs is a limited world, and there is both comfort and peace in limitation. There is also acceptance.

PP: What do you mean by acceptance?

MM: I mean that society approves.

PP: And society *doesn't* approve of your kind of woman?

MM: Not particularly. We are admired when we are successful, but otherwise women who have a working existence of their own are excused as needing the money, or tacitly deplored as neglecting their human obligations.

PP: Isn't this sometimes the case?

MM: Of course it is; and what you call 'career women' have a much tougher time meeting their human obligations than nesting females. But if we are not ideal mothers or ideal wives, it does not follow that they always are either.

PP: What do you mean by "nesting females"?

MM: Exactly what I said: little bodies all settled on moss and twigs, tugging at pieces of string. No, seriously, I find something lacking in the woman who fails to emerge from her nest even when the fledglings are grown. Her horizons are narrowed and her resources are thin. And her conversation is a grab-bag of personal and domestic trivia.

PP: Don't you think that career women can be boring too?

MM: Most certainly yes—when they take themselves too seriously and get too intense about what *they* are doing.

But if they're any good at all, they have more to say than the obsessive housewife who can talk of nothing but slip-covers, bargains, and Junior's cold.

PP: Are you then saying that you think *all* women should have jobs outside their home?

MM: Not jobs. Interests. Interests that have nothing to do with the mechanisms of the home.

PP: What about their husbands. Don't they prefer home-bodies?

MM: They may think they do. But an awful lot of husbands take cover behind their newspapers and seal their ears against the torrent of small troubles of homebound wives.

PP: I gather from everything you say that you are not domestic?

MM: The things you people gather! On the contrary, I love my home. I love making it pleasant. I love to cook. But I cannot for the life of me see how, after children are grown, this can be a full-time occupation. And I strongly suspect that the women who make such heavy weather about housework organize badly, or are compulsively attached to small perfections. They don't have to meet deadlines.

PP: What do you mean by that?

MM: I mean that professional women are better at planning their time because they have to. If they don't, they're no good at the job.

PP: Let's get back to you again. How *do* you manage to combine your work and your home without sacrificing either?

MM: Aha, the old question! And the old answer: I don't. You can't manage without some sacrifice. I don't think there's any greater conflict than this tangle of loyalties. You have to maintain a painfully delicate equilibrium of loves and duties. This needs perpetual flexibility—vision—adjustment.

PP: You make it sound very hard.

MM: It *is* very hard. It's hard for a man too. But he has help: a wife to shield him at home, and a secretary to sustain him at work. We have neither.

PP: But career women have secretaries, haven't they?

MM: Office women, yes . . . organization women. But I am talking about women like myself, who work in some creative field of their own. We are exposed to every intrusion, at all times.

PP: Can't you shut the door?

MM: You can shut the door but you can't shut out a sick husband or a troubled child. And you can't shut out the practical demands of even a small household: food to be ordered, clothes to be cleaned—and the sorrows of your part-time cleaning woman to be listened to.

PP: Can't you simply refuse these things, or delegate them?

MM: Refuse concern? Delegate compassion? No, not if you are a human being. There is nothing harder to come by than detachment and solitude; and nothing more important.

PP: *Nothing* more important?

MM: Not to the mind, or what one calls the soul. I don't think any man or any woman can be whole without these hours—of abstraction, of contemplation, of self-discovery. I suppose this is why I find the whole concept of group-living so repellent, whether it is in a Soviet society or one of our own suburb communities.

PP: You sound antisocial. Are you?

MM: You can call me that if you want. I would prefer "anti-joiner."

PP: Meaning what?

MM: Meaning that I'm not particularly happy belonging to—or being identified with—any one group. I don't like labels or doctrines. In a purely Jewish society I yearn for Christians, in a purely Christian society I miss Jews. Among socially "right" people, I feel radical, and among radicals I feel conservative.

PP: What about your own field, writing? Don't you belong to any group there?

MM: If I do, I'd like to know what it is.

PP: Miss Mannes, as a professional do you find yourself equal to men?

MM: If you mean, do I think I am as good as some men in my field, yes.

PP: What about those men? Do they accept you as an equal, although you are a woman?

MM: Why don't you ask *them?*

PP: What about the public at large? Is there any discrimination there?

MM: To a certain degree. As a woman you have to be extremely successful to be considered important by most people: a Claire Boothe Luce, a national institution like Eleanor Roosevelt—or the author of *Peyton Place*. But I think conventional society is the most guilty of discrimination.

PP: Why? How would you explain that, if it is true?

MM: Because the arbiters of that society, the hostesses, are women. And they are the last to recognize and acknowledge professional distinction in other women . . . especially if they know them.

PP: You sound as if you had suffered at their hands?

MM: 'Suffered' is too strong a word. Let's say they keep trying to put you in your place, which is really their own.

PP: I don't follow you—

MM: They acknowledge only your social identity as a wife; not your personal identity as a writer. It is so much easier to introduce couples than individuals: two roles for one woman are a bore!

PP: Do you think jealousy plays any part in this?

MM: Partly. But it's mostly convention. In their world, achievements are part of a man's identity. But a woman's achievements are accessories—to be noticed or not . . . and not to be taken too seriously.

PP: Do *you* take them seriously?

MM: Of course—in other women as well as in myself. They're an integral part of us.

PP: (*after a long draw at a cigarette and with an air of summation*) Miss Mannes, from everything you have said tonight, your conclusion seems to be that career women are the noblest acts of God, the jewels in the crown of our society, the paragons of the female sex, superior to all others in all ways. Do you care to comment on that?

MM: I certainly do. I would like to introduce you to two very different career women: products of fiction but aspects of reality!

Lady editor

Only the United States and only the twentieth century could produce a woman like Constance Maybie, and only one adjective does her justice: remarkable. For Connie is a multiple being, living a number of lives each one of which, in other times and places, would have sufficed one woman from birth to death. She is the editor of a nationwide woman's magazine, a TV guest, a smart dresser, a good cook, an excellent hostess, a mother, and a wife, in that order.

To the uninitiated, the metamorphoses from one life to another are dazzling. One moment Connie will be sitting in her large office (cinnamon and gray, the flowers always white), a small hat on her head, talking on one of three telephones, now crisp, now rapturous, now tough; another she will be lunching with a famous obstetrician to plan the third article of a medical series, this one to be "Am I Sterile?" (Connie now the serious technical woman); later, looking a little older and harder than she is, she will be giving out graciousness and recipes for curried shrimp on a TV woman's program; later again that night you can find her entertaining eight distinguished people in her Regency apartment, drawing them out on missiles and Nasser; and still later Connie the wife will be calling good night to her husband Horace as he pads to his bedroom across the hall from hers.

Connie the mother is visible only on vacations and for a few weeks in summer, for her daughter Christine is at Smith and needs maternal attention only in those areas which affect her appearance and her social integration. Connie and Christine have posed a number of times in mother-and-daughter-like-sisters features in the fashion magazine belonging to the same publishers who print her own *Woman's Hour,* dedicated to better homes and minds in the thirty-to-fifty age bracket. Truly a remarkable woman.

Even more remarkable is the fact that Constance Maybie does not have to do all the things she does or be as busy as she is or earn twenty-five thousand a year. Horace had a pleasant income from a family industry when she married him and has since inherited an even pleasanter one and a house in Fairfield upon the death of his mother three years ago. But, fond as she is of Horace—and she is very, very fond—he has never been enough for her. His pleasant manners, good breeding, and country-squire appearance have been consistently valuable to her as "background," relieving her—as does the simple white house— of the stigma of careerism and sophistication inconsistent with the wholesome suburban aims of *Woman's Hour.*

But because Horace has little vitality and no ambition, his company is inclined to be enervating and his conversation—devoted largely to bird watching—boring to herself and her friends. Connie has never permitted herself this adjective, playing up as she does to "Horace's passion" by giving him expensive bird books as soon as they

are published and diverting the conversation at least once
an evening to migration. "Darling," she will say, "tell
about those fascinating grosbeaks!" She is also very con-
siderate in putting her young and inexperienced editors
next to him at dinner, partly because they think it is an
honor and partly to save her important guests for each
other. These, having once gone through the amenities of
meeting Connie's husband, seldom bother to speak to him
again. In public they refer to the Maybies as a charming
couple, usually adding, "and she's so wonderful with
him," as if he were a dog, or sick. In private they say,
"Poor Connie." Only the young and tender or the old
and wise say, "Poor Horace." Somewhere along the line,
they feel, Horace could have become a man.

Whatever they think, people are forced to admire Constance Maybie for doing so much so well. *Woman's Hour*
has never had more advertising or higher circulation or
been more courageous in every field except the political,
where its publishers consider an interview with Madame
Pandit as far to the left as they dare go. Otherwise, Connie's policy has been one of unparalleled frankness. Few
diseases, few human conditions or emotions have escaped
its pages, and the faithful subscriber is now conditioned
to finding a study of incest tucked between fall fashions
and the confession of a nymphomaniac drug addict following an article on new uses for oilcloth. There is no
thought of sensationalism in this; to use Connie's words,
"women are people"—they deserve to know all.

They must also, and this is to Connie Maybie's lasting
credit, feel all. No appeal, whether for Arab children or
the prevention of forest fires, has been denied her edi-
toral help, and a separate cabinet in her office is filled
with medals and citations of gratitude for her efforts.

What, then, is wrong about this remarkable woman, who works so hard and looks so well and leads a life of complete fulfillment? Nothing, really. If someone should ask whether Horace is really happy or whether Christine really loves her mother, the answers can be that Horace has not complained and that Christine is doing very well at Smith. Has Connie not made an attractive home for them? Does she not give them all she has—left over?

If one were to persist, one could find one other area of doubt. If Connie were ever to apply to herself the clinical attention which her magazine bestows on others, she would find one of the most dependent creatures in the world; dependent on people, dependent on things, dependent even on Horace. Constance Maybie can only do; she cannot be. Her identity is the sum of parts which, oddly enough, do not make up a whole.

The marriage

Jessie Burnside was very happily married. Her husband was a plain office desk and she loved him. He and Jessie were so much one, in fact, that she embodied a contemporary and female species of a centaur: half woman, half desk. Without her mahogany half she was the loneliest woman in the world, and the least complete. That is why she hated week ends and holidays: they were intolerable absences from love. And that is why Monday mornings, for so many miserable, were for her rapturous returns.

If the pretty young file clerks and typists in her office knew more about Jessie's life, they would not have tittered among themselves at her unnatural zeal; and they might have understood, at least a little, why she came to work at eight-thirty and stayed until six and never went down for coffee.

For Jessie Burnside lived with an arthritic mother in a drab apartment near Riverside Drive, without sight of the river. That noble sweep might have been some compensation for her mother's furniture, her mother's complaints, and the long subway rides morning and night. But at fifty-three Jessie had long since ceased to speculate on any other way of life. Ever since her father had died twenty years ago she had been trapped; by the helplessness of her mother, by her own ethics, and by her painful shyness with men. Only in the presence of her husband, her desk, could she deal with them. Then, and only then, was she calm, assured and poised; a woman who knew people, an able director of personnel. Away from him she was a dim old maid, living with her mother.

The desk was a good husband: it supported her, amused her, and kept her company. The In Tray was its brain, always unpredictable, endlessly fascinating. It brought people and ideas into her life. It was a challenge and a stimulation, for which the Out Tray, her own intelligence, was a perfect match.

Never did woman straighten her husband's tie with more care and tenderness than Jessie arranged her desk. Never were clothes pressed and laid out with more love and attention than Jessie gave to fresh stacks of paper and envelopes and clips and memo-pads. Every morning the serene and polished countenance of her husband looked up at her gratefully. Every evening she composed it again for the long night of separation. At six, when life began for nearly all the men and women who worked in Jessie's company, life was suspended for her. The evening subway ride took her away; not toward.

The corollary of any devotion as intense as this is usually jealousy. And this was true of Jessie and her husband. She lived in constant and corroding fear that her desk, her job, would be taken from her by someone else; someone younger, more competent, more attractive. So she did what some women do to keep their husbands faithful to them: she never let her desk out of her sight. In this she was aided by a constitution so sound that she had taken sick leave only twice in fifteen years, and then only for three-day intervals; and by the utter lack of conflicting interests.

The pretty young typists called Jessie a stick, a drip, a grind. The young advertising men respected her but thanked God they were men, and young. The director of the company had just about made up his mind to get some new blood into the firm. Burnside was a good old drag, but Christ, what legs. Also, it had become increasingly clear that Jessie was making life miserable for the pretty young things. Their squawks about her discriminations confirmed his belief that efficiency coupled with bad morale was no longer efficiency.

So one morning the boss called Jessie Burnside into his office and said, "Miss Burnside, as you may know we're going through a sort of reorganization here. Our budget's been slashed again and we've got to make cuts all down the line. Mr. Wasey's office is going to take over personnel, and that puts us into a terrible spot about you, Miss Burnside. . . ."

The boss looked at her with what he felt was his boyish grin, but Jessie was silent.

"You've done a wonderful job all these years and the last thing we want to do is to let you down. So don't worry, we're planning to pay your full salary through the year, and then of course, your pension. . . ."

Jessie then spoke, her voice trembling slightly, her face very dry and white.

"It's Miss Carver, isn't it?"

"What was that, Miss Burnside?" asked the boss, leaning forward over his desk.

In a louder voice she said, "It's that Miss Carver, isn't it . . . she's going to take my job."

"Good heavens, no, Miss Burnside, there's no thought of that—why, Miss Carver's just Mr. Wasey's secretary." Lucky bastard, added the boss to himself.

"She's always wanted my job," said Jessie, "always! I've seen her snooping around my office, my desk!" she cried, rising and shaking. "You can't fool me!"

It was a painful session and it took the boss quite a while to calm her down. He did this by lying that the re-organization was not imminent, that no changes would be made for at least three months. He was sweating pro-fusely when she finally left the office.

His relief was short-lived, however. That same night, at nine o'clock in the deserted building, the watchman found Jessie Burnside trying to move her desk out of the office into the corridor. He said that she was making no sense at all.

But he was wrong, of course. Jessie Burnside was mak-ing perfect sense. No one else was going to take her hus-band from her. She'd see to that, if it was the last thing she did.

6

MEDITATIONS IN AN EMPTY ROOM

In a corner of the curve of the UN General Assembly Building is a small place called the Meditation Room—built in 1952, according to a small plaque, and furnished by public contribution. It is windowless and rectangular, but rounded at one end, curtained from floor to ceiling in off-white, carpeted in off-white, and lit by beams from spotlights in the ceiling. It has since been redecorated, but when I saw it about twenty armchairs of American pine with barrel-stave backs, five to a row, faced the curved end of the room, in the center of which was a polished reddish tree trunk about four feet high and three feet across; and on top of that was a cluster of philodendron in a receptacle. A separate shaft of light was directed on this, as if it were significant.

The room was empty. I tried to think what it reminded me of. The basement lounge of a small movie theater? The showroom of a wholesale fur designer? But they are not so claustrophobic.

The information desk told me that the room was conceived and executed by the Laymen's Movement for a Christian World, as a place of communion or worship, where men might pray or ponder in peace, preparing themselves for that verbal battle of attrition, that exploration of hope, which is the UN. And since it was for the use of scores of nations and many religions, the mandate was clear to avoid any symbol that might offend any believer. Even the United Nations flag, once there, had had to be removed. So now there were the trunk, the plant, and the chairs.

It seemed to me standing there that this nothingness was so oppressive and disturbing that it became a sort of madness, and the room a sort of padded cell. It seemed to me that the core of our greatest contemporary trouble lay here, that all this whiteness and shapelessness and weakness was the leukemia of noncommitment, sapping our strength. We had found, finally, that only nothing could please all, and we were trying to make the greatest of all generalities out of that most singular truth, the spirit of man. The terrifying thing about this room was that it made no statement whatever. In its opacity and constriction, it could not even act as a reflector of thought.

Outside, in the city, I began to see this noncommitment everywhere. I looked at the new buildings, the glassy aluminum boxes rising everywhere in place of the old. They made no statement. They offended no one. They had no stamp upon them. They were faceless. This was the kind of taste that is no taste, not even bad taste.

I thought of hour upon hour and month upon month of radio and television, produced to please all by offending none. The people who commanded audiences of thirty to fifty million, men like Perry Como and Ed Sullivan, did so because at no time did they commit themselves to anything but their sponsors' products. Once in a blue moon a play would make a statement, only to retract or temper it in a show of neutrality. It takes an ultimate act of adjustment—the twin of conformity—to make sixty million people look at the same thing at the same time. And they do, nearly every day.

That is why any statement, any commitment of self, is a stab of joy, on television or anywhere else—a rush of plasma into the draining bloodstream of our condition. And that is why gratitude is due to those quiet conversations with men and women on television series such as NBC's "Wisdom," whose entire lives have been statements of their singularity. You have only to look at their faces—Arnold Toynbee, Bertrand Russell, Edward Steichen, Pablo Casals, Robert Frost, Jawaharlal Nehru, Wanda Landowska—to see how their features have been cast in the forge of the spirit's privacy, how immeasurably removed they are—in time, alas, as well as in form—from all of us. And when the great cellist Casals—a little stubborn round-shouldered man in a sweater—says in difficult English that he will never stand for the kind of political immorality that tolerates Franco; when Nehru speaks without rancor of his eight years in prison, a most tangible commitment; when Robert Oppenheimer (on his memorable interview with Murrow on CBS) gently tries to define truth, his face illuminated by the search; when Russell dares to be quizzical about accepted values and attitudes—then we know what we are missing every day of our lives in the pallid company of the uncommittted.

In his last book entitled *Must You Conform?* the late psychiatrist Robert Lindner presented one cure for this spiritual leukemia: "I suggest that the answer . . . lies in the mobilization and implementation of the instinct of rebellion. We must, in short, become acquainted with our protestant nature and learn how to use it in our daily lives, how to express it ourselves, how to infuse it throughout all levels of our culture, and how to nourish it in our young."

If we don't, presumably the spirit of man will be both represented and worshiped in rooms like this one in the UN—a quiet place of detachment where we can look at the philodendron in their light from nowhere and meditate on nothing.

Yet if someone were to say that the only salvation from this void was a commitment to God and to the doctrines and practices of a formal religion, I would demur. For I feel a basic commitment even though I belong to no denomination and no church. Since I am neither of the Catholic nor Jewish faith, I suppose I am Protestant; yet that is not strictly correct because I have not been baptized. I would call myself Christian if that meant, simply, that I believed in Christ.

If I were asked, moreover, if I believed in God, I would say that I did not know. I believe in a grand universal order and meaning, and I believe in a power that is both greater than us and within us. But I do not think I believe in the God that is worshiped formally in churches, a God that answers prayers, that guides and shapes, that comforts and chides, that is—when you really come down to it —a benevolent and all-seeing entity built recognizably in man's image. I certainly do not believe in the God that is invoked by our public characters as an ally in righteousness. He would be a shabby God indeed.

But I do believe in a great many things that the formal worshipers of God profess to believe, and they are not abstracts but the highest purposes for which man exists. To believe, with passion, in justice, in kindness, in decency, in humility, in courage and in honor, it is not necessary to believe in God. It is necessary only to be fully aware of the magnificence of the universe and the wonder of man himself, both part of a cosmic pattern revealed equally in a raindrop and the chorales of Johann Sebastian Bach.

It may well have been music, in fact, that gave me whatever religion—if that is the word—sustains me. Music first, then the works of man in other forms, and then—not least but latest—the natural world. These wonders I can worship, with no other reference. Because they are greater than any human identity they need not be given a name. They are enough.

What can a minister give me that Beethoven cannot? What can a church give me that a Piero della Francesca cannot? What can a sermon give me that I cannot find in a Shakespeare sonnet or the lines of the great philosophers and poets? What can church ritual give me that great dance cannot? All these creative acts of man lift, shrive, and enlarge man. When I listen to these things and see these things, my humility is balanced by a prodigious urge towards light, towards a state of grace. In them I see purpose and pattern, and seeing them, a way to arrive at them. Pettiness falls away, supplanted by compassion. Who, hearing and seeing these things, can bear to destroy?

So, too, can the shape of a leaf or the palpitating body of a bird or the swell of a cumulus cloud be of infinite succor. They are all marvelous and full of meaning, which is life itself. What can be found in a church that is greater than these things or composed of half their perfection?

One thing only, I think: the words of Christ. And I for one would far rather read them in solitude than hear them intoned and explained in company. I doubt if any greater disservice has been done to Christ than the manner in which his teachings have been presented in a thousand pulpits: self-righteously, mournfully, nasally, coldly, feebly, flamboyantly, cozily, blandly, violently. And if you have forgotten what it can be like in church, turn your radio on some Sunday and hear how a man can desecrate Christ.

I know, of course, that there are ministers who give the Gospel its full beauty and power and meaning. I know there are many thousands of good, honest, serious people who derive guidance and comfort from listening to them. And I know that there is a deep human need for some spiritual form—and formality—in a society so lacking in social form. They appear to need, too, a sense of communion with others in sharing this form. They cannot arrive at a single vision by themselves: others must define and support their truth.

I respect these people even if I am not of them. But I would respect the church more if it could breathe life into its forms, grown perfunctory and pallid with long acceptance. I would respect it more if it could impose real disciplines on its congregations instead of a weekly show of piety. To paraphrase the song from *Porgy and Bess* about women, "religion is a sometime thing" in America now, and the gap between formal faith and informal behavior has never been wider in any society. As a people we claim a Christian morality while we condone, in business and in life, the grossest dishonesties. No man is a Christian who cheats his fellows, perverts the truth, or speaks of a "clean bomb"; yet he will be the first to make public his faith in God.

This marriage of form and substance, then, is what I have not found in today's church. I have found, moreover, religious forms which deeply offend my own perceptions of life and death. Funerals are for me pagan and abhorrent, for in their emphasis on physical dissolution, they perform a burial of the spirit. The blackness, the casket, the pallbearers, the weeping faces of the bereaved or of vicarious grievers—what have these to do with man's triumphant procedure? And what greater indecency than exposing a treated corpse to public view? Aside from the state funerals of the great, which are historical pageants that give shape to public mourning, I remember only one funeral that seemed to me right. This took place many years ago on a Spanish island in the Bay of Biscay, and it consisted only of this: a girl in bright clothes holding aloft a small casket of ashes and followed by a band. The procession was a gay and celebrative dance, as if death had conferred a favor on life. And those who grieved in their hearts were not in view.

But there is little sense of joy or celebration in our churches, and far too little beauty. Either they have a bleakness which is closer to paucity than purity, or a quality of gimcrackery provided by bad religious art and artifacts, than which no art can be worse. There is no reason why a church should be ugly and every reason why it should be beautiful. There is every reason, too, why a minister, of all men, should be a master of speech. But art and the church have for too long deserted each other. And the most encouraging sign in the church for years is the evidence that it is beginning to find this out. If it cannot be revitalized from within, perhaps it can be revitalized from without. And some of the new designs for churches are doing just that.

For the time being, however, I will continue to stay away from them. I will listen, rather, to Gluck's *Orpheus* or dive into the curve of foaming breakers on a deserted shore. I am committed to these ecstasies.

Above all, let me never—in some future adversity—cry for comfort and sustenance to a God I never before addressed, but to the best and strongest within myself.